T0318146

ARCHITEKTEN REISEN

DESIGN-REFUGIEN AN DER OSTSEE

WHERE ARCHITECTS STAY AT THE BALTIC SEA

LODGINGS FOR DESIGN ENTHUSIASTS

SIBYLLE KRAMER

ARCHITEKTEN REISEN

DESIGN-REFUGIEN AN DER OSTSEE

WHERE ARCHITECTS STAY AT THE BALTIC SEA

LODGINGS FOR DESIGN ENTHUSIASTS

BRAUN

The Deutsche Nationalbibliothek lists this publication in the Deutsche Nationalbibliografie; detailed bibliographic data are available on the Internet at http://dnb.dnb.de

ISBN 978-3-3-03768-281-4
© 2023 by Braun Publishing AG
www.braun-publishing.ch

1st edition 2023

Editor: Sibylle Kramer
Editorial staff and layout:
Alessia Calabrò
Translation: Sandra Ellegiers
Graphic concept: Michaela Prinz, Berlin
Reproduction: Bild1Druck GmbH, Berlin

Die Deutsche Nationalbibliothek verzeichnet diese Publikation in der Deutschen Nationalbibliografie; detaillierte bibliografische Daten sind im Internet über http://dnb.dnb.de abrufbar.

ISBN 978-3-3-03768-281-4
© 2023 Braun Publishing AG
www.braun-publishing.ch

Dieses Werk ist urheberrechtlich geschützt. Jede Verwendung außerhalb der engen Grenzen des Urheberrechtsgesetzes, der keine Berechtigung durch den Verlag erteilt wurde, ist unbefugt und strafbar. Dies gilt insbesondere für Vervielfältigungen, Übersetzungen, Mikroverfilmung und das Abspeichern oder die Verarbeitung in elektronischen Systemen.

1. Auflage 2023

Redaktion: Sibylle Kramer
Mitarbeit Redaktion und Layout:
Alessia Calabrò
Übersetzung: Sandra Ellegiers
Grafisches Konzept: Michaela Prinz, Berlin
Reproduktion: Bild1Druck GmbH, Berlin

Alle Informationen in diesem Band wurden mit dem besten Gewissen der Redaktion zusammengestellt. Das Buch basiert auf den Informationen, die der Verlag von Architekten- und Designbüros erhielt und schließt jegliche Haftung aus. Der Verlag übernimmt keine Verantwortung für die Richtigkeit und Vollständigkeit sowie Urheberrechte und verweist auf die angegebenen Quellen (Architekten- und Designbüros sowie Betreiber). Alle Rechte an den Fotografien sind im Besitz der Fotografen (siehe Abbildungsnachweise).

Contents
Inhalt

Contents
Inhalt

Living and dining area of HAUS ZWEINEUN.
Exterior view of Vipp Chimney House.
Wohn- und Essbereich HAUS ZWEINEUN.
Außenansicht Vipp Chimney House.

Preface
Vorwort

The combination of architecture and vacation is an auspicious one. Relaxation and enjoyment in a perfectly designed environment hardly leave anything to be desired. After the success of the previous volumes, this new book, focusing on the Baltic Sea, responds to readers' requests for a geographically denser architectural travel guide covering the Baltic coasts of Germany, Denmark, and Sweden. The Baltic Sea's coast is characterized by many varieties of seascapes, wide sandy beaches with colorful beach chairs, fashionable seaside resorts, impressive chalk cliffs, and tall lighthouses.

The current book features 45 charming and masterfully designed architectural properties on the coast and in its nearby inland, by lakes and in towns. Being surrounded by the beautiful nature, the power of the water and inspiring Hanseatic or design cities, these are great places to organize amazing road trips. In addition to the wonderful tranquility of nature, the coast and the rural inland offer excellent conditions for water sports and hiking, while cities such as Copenhagen, Lübeck and Malmö are the perfect spots to enjoy culture, design, and urban activities. Even those who prefer staying in one place for a longer period will find an exceptional temporary home among the selected, in terms of architecture unique accommodations. Whether you sleep in an historic manor house of an old estate, in a former industrial crane in the harbor, in a rustic farm cottage by the lake, high up in the air in a tree house or in a small and fine solitary home in a sheep pasture, you will always find yourself in a wonderful environment rich in attractions.

Discover the Baltic Sea coast in a whole new way ...

Exterior view of KAJ Hotel. Gut Üselitz.
Barn House interior view.
Außenansicht KAJ Hotel. Gut Üselitz.
Innenansicht Barn House.

Architektur und Urlaub ist eine verheißungsvolle Verbindung. Erholung und Genuss in einer vollendet gestalteten Umgebung lassen nur wenige Wünsche offen. Nach dem Erfolg der vorherigen Bände, entspricht dieses neue, auf die Ostsee fokussierte Buch, den Wünschen der Leser nach einem geografisch dichteren Architekturreiseführer für die Ostseeküste der Länder Deutschland, Dänemark und Schweden. Vielseitiges Meer, weite Sandstrände mit bunten Strandkörben, mondäne Seebäder, imposante Kreidefelsen und hohe Leuchttürme prägen die Bilder dieser Küste. Das aktuelle Buch zeigt 45 bezaubernde und architektonisch gekonnt gestaltete Objekte an der Küste und im nahen Binnenland, an Seen und in Städten. Umgeben von der wunderschönen Natur, der Kraft des Wassers und inspirierenden Hanse- oder Design-Städten lassen sich wunderbare Roadtrips organisieren. Die Küste und das ländliche Binnenland bieten neben der wunderbaren Ruhe der Natur beste Wassersport- und Wanderbedingungen, in Städten wie Kopenhagen, Lübeck und Malmö lassen sich Kultur, Design und urbane Aktivitäten genießen. Auch wer lieber länger an einem Ort verweilt, findet unter den ausgewählten, architektonisch besonderen Unterkünften ein außergewöhnliches Zuhause auf Zeit. Ob Sie im historischen Herrenhaus einer alten Gutsanlage, in einem alten Industriekran im Hafen, in einer urigen Bauernkate am See, in luftiger Höhe im Baumhaus oder im kleinen und feinen Solitaire auf der Schafweide schlafen, Sie befinden sich stets in einer wunderbaren Umgebung, die viel zu bieten hat. Entdecken Sie die Ostseeküste auf eine ganz neue Art und Weise ...

INFORMATION. ARCHITECTS> ATELIER SUNDER-PLASSMANN // 2021. HOUSE> 55 SQM // 4 GUESTS // 2 SLEEPING BERTHS // 1 BATHROOM. ADDRESS> WACHOLDERWEG 1, KAPPELN, GERMANY. WWW.FERIENHAUS-HOF-AHMEN.DE

Exterior view from the garden. Kitchen area with panoramic view. Bunk bed.
Außenansicht vom Garten. Küchenbereich mit Panoramablick. Schlafkoje.

Ferienhaus Hof Ahmen

KAPPELN, GERMANY |
DEUTSCHLAND

Set in the isolated sheep pasture of a listed farm, a new house was built using unique, modern architecture. The spacious main room is glazed on three sides, blurring the lines between landscape and architecture, rustic and modern, interior and exterior. Balancing these elements carefully defines its design. In addition to the living-dining area and kitchen with counter, the house is equipped with two separate, cozy wood-paneled bunks. Otherwise, the interior is kept neat and minimalist and does not distract from the real protagonist – the impressive nature.

Auf der abgeschiedenen Schafweide eines denkmalgeschützten Hofes wurde ein Neubau mit eigenständiger, moderner Architektur errichtet. Der großzügige Hauptraum ist dreiseitig verglast und lässt die Grenzen zwischen Landschaft und Architektur, zwischen Ländlich und Modern, zwischen Innen und Außen verschmelzen. Das behutsame Austarieren und Ausbalancieren dieser Elemente bestimmen den Entwurf. Neben Wohn-Essbereich und Küche mit Tresen ist das Haus mit zwei abtrennbaren, gemütlichen holzverkleideten Schlafkojen ausgestattet. Ansonsten ist das Interieur pur und minimalistisch gehalten und lenkt nicht ab vom eigentlichen Hauptdarsteller – der eindrucksvollen Natur.

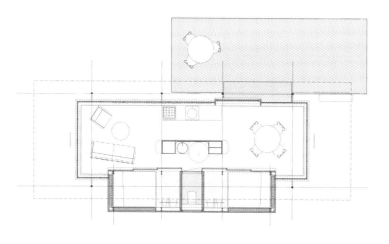

GETTING AROUND. CLOSE TO SCHLEI RIVER THERE ARE MANY PLACES TO VISIT: E. G. THE LANDESMUSEUM IN SCHLESWIG, FOR CHILDREN THE PHÄNOMENTA IN FLENSBURG, THE SMALL TOWNS OF ARNIS OR KAPPELN WITH MANY SHOPPING POSSIBILITIES. THE BALTIC SEA BEACH WEIDEFELD AND THE STEEP COAST IN SCHÖNHAGEN ARE BOTH ABOUT FIVE KILOMETERS AWAY. HIKERS AND NATURE LOVERS WILL ENJOY THE GELTINGER BIRK, REESHOLM AND SCHLEIMÜNDE.

IN DER UMGEBUNG. RUND UM DIE SCHLEI GIBT ES ZAHLREICHE AUSFLUGSZIELE: Z. B. DAS LANDESMUSEUM IN SCHLESWIG, FÜR KINDER DIE PHÄNOMENTA IN FLENSBURG, DIE KLEINEN STÄDTE ARNIS ODER KAPPELN MIT VIELEN EINKAUFSMÖGLICHKEITEN. DER OSTSEESTRAND WEIDEFELD UND DIE STEILKÜSTE IN SCHÖNHAGEN SIND JEWEILS FÜNF KM ENTFERNT. FÜR WANDERER UND NATURLIEBHABER SIND DIE GELTINGER BIRK, REESHOLM UND SCHLEIMÜNDE INTERESSANT.

Exterior view in the evening.
Floor plan. Dining area.
Außenansicht mit Abendstimmung.
Grundriss. Essbereich.

Interior view. Detail of the kitchen.
Exterior view of the entrance.
Innenansicht. Detail Küche.
Außenbereich des Eingangs.

INFORMATION. ARCHITECTS>
DIVE ARCHITECTS // 2018.
HOUSE> 560 SQM // APARTMENT
5 GUESTS, STUDIO 3 GUESTS
AND CABIN 3 GUESTS //
1–3 BEDROOMS EACH UNIT //
1 BATHROOM EACH UNIT.
ADDRESS> BYADAMMSVÄGEN 33,
SIMRIS, SWEDEN.
WWW.GRAMSGARD.SE

Exterior view. View of the stairs.
Interior view of the living room.
Außenansicht. Blick auf die Treppe.
Innenansicht Wohnzimmer.

Dining and kitchen area. Interior view.
Grams Gård atmosphere in the evening.
Ess- und Küchenbereich. Innenansicht.
Grams Gård mit Abendstimmung.

Grams Gård

SIMRIS, SWEDEN | SCHWEDEN

Grams Gård farm was built in 1851. It is located on a small hill overlooking the sea and consists of three structures constituting a courtyard with cobblestones and a large chestnut tree. The project is characterized by combining tradition and innovation as well as a fine sense of materials. Black roofs, white stone walls and some old preserved windows meet large window openings, oak, stone and concrete floors. Plenty of natural light enters the rooms through windows, revealing views of the garden and fields. Skylights brighten and heat the rooms on the second floor, three large dormers open to the landscape. The first floor apartment of 90 sqm and the second floor studio of 50 sqm feature walls in pale colors and understated furnishings with colorful accents.

Der Hof Grams Gård wurde 1851 erbaut. Er liegt auf einer kleinen Anhöhe mit Blick auf das Meer und besteht aus drei Baukörpern, die einen Hof mit Kopfsteinpflaster und großem Kastanienbaum bilden. Die Kombination aus Tradition und Innovation und ein feiner Sinn für Materialien prägen das Projekt. Schwarze Dächer, weiße Steinwände und einige alte, erhaltene Fenster treffen auf große Fensteröffnungen, Eichen-, Stein- und Betonböden. Fenster lassen viel Licht in die Räume und geben den Blick auf den Garten und die Felder frei. Die Oberlichter erhellen und erwärmen die Räume im Obergeschoss, drei große Dachgauben öffnen sich zur Landschaft. Das Apartment im Erdgeschoss mit 90 qm und das Studio mit 50 qm im ersten Stock sind mit hellen Wänden und einer zurückhaltenden Möblierung mit farbigen Akzenten gestaltet.

Front exterior view.
Interior view of the kitchen.
Außenansicht.
Innenansicht der Küche.

*Gallery on the second floor. Grams Gård from
the garden. Interior view. Floor plan.
Galerie im ersten Obergeschoss. Grams Gård vom
Garten aus. Innenansicht. Grundriss.*

GETTING AROUND. THE FARM
OFFERS BOTH TRANQUILITY AND
PROXIMITY TO THE COASTAL TOWNS
OF SIMRISHAMN AND BRANTEVIK. IT
TAKES ONLY FIVE MINUTES BY BIKE
TO GET TO THE WATER AND ENJOY A
REFRESHING SWIM. THE WHITE SANDY
BEACHES OF THE SANDHAMMAREN
NATURE RESERVE CAN BE REACHED
BY CAR IN 25 MINUTES.

IN DER UMGEBUNG. DER HOF
BIETET SOWOHL RUHE ALS AUCH
DIE NÄHE ZU DEN KÜSTENSTÄDTEN
SIMRISHAMN UND BRANTEVIK. IN NUR
FÜNF MINUTEN GELANGT MAN MIT
DEM FAHRRAD ZUM WASSER UND
KANN HIER EIN ERFRISCHENDES BAD
GENIESSEN. IN 25 MINUTEN ERREICHT
MAN MIT DEM AUTO DIE WEISSEN
SANDSTRÄNDE DES SANDHAMMAREN
NATURRESERVATS.

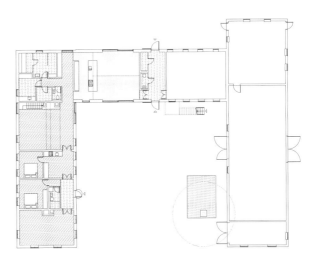

INFORMATION. ARCHITECTS>
PLH ARKITEKTER // 1800S ARTISTS'
GUESTHOUSE, RENOVATION 2019.
BOUTIQUE HOTEL> 700 SQM //
6 APARTMENTS FOR 2 GUESTS WITH
THE POSSIBILITY OF AN EXTRA BED,
1 APARTMENT FOR 4 GUESTS AND
1 DOUBLE ROOM APARTMENT WITH
AN OPEN FLOOR PLAN HANDICAP
FRIENDLY // 1 BATHROOM EACH.
ADDRESS> LANGEBJERGVEJ 1,
BORRE, DENMARK.
WWW.VILLAHUNO.COM

View of Villa Huno from the garden. Exterior view.
Interior view of one of the apartments.
Blick auf Villa Huno vom Garten. Außenansicht.
Innenansicht einer Wohnung.

Villa Huno

MØN, DENMARK | DÄNEMARK

Hunosøgaard was built at the end of the 19th century as a guesthouse for artists. The historic building was transformed into Villa Huno, a modern boutique hotel and gourmet restaurant in midst of nature. Villa Huno is located in the UNESCO biosphere reserve of Møn, off the beaten path, surrounded by a beautiful old beech forest and on the edge of Lake Hunosø. Its architecture is inspired by traditional Danish farmhouses, using natural materials such as larch façades and sedum roofs. Each of the hotel's eight apartments has panoramic windows with seats incorporated in the frame, bringing light, air and nature into the rooms. Villa Huno is accessible to everyone and equipped with universal, inclusive facilities.

Hunosøgaard wurde Ende des 19. Jahrhunderts als Gästehaus für Künstler gebaut. Nun wurde das historische Gebäude in die Villa Huno umgewandelt, ein modernes Boutiquehotel und Gourmet-Restaurant – mitten in der Natur. Im UNESCO-Biosphärenreservat Møn liegt die Villa Huno abseits der ausgetretenen Pfade, umgeben von einem wunderschönen alten Buchenwald und am Rande des Hunosø-Sees. Die Architektur ist an traditionelle dänische Bauernhäuser angelehnt, mit natürlichen Materialien wie Lärchenfassaden und Sedumdächern. Jedes der acht Apartments des Hotels verfügt über Panoramafenster mit in den Rahmen eingebauten Sitzgelegenheiten, die Licht, Luft und Natur in die Räume bringen. Die Villa Huno ist für jedermann zugänglich und mit universellen, inklusiven Einrichtungen ausgestattet.

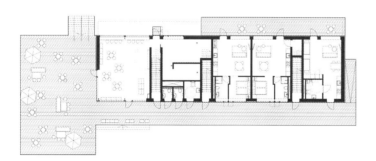

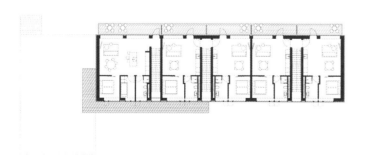

GETTING AROUND. MØN'S MAIN ATTRACTION IS THE FAMOUS CHALK CLIFFS MØNS KLINT. IF YOU WANT TO DIVE DEEP INTO GEOLOGICAL HISTORY, VISIT THE INTERACTIVE NATURAL HISTORY MUSEUM GEO-CENTER MØNS KLINT, ALSO BY PLH ARKITEKTER. IT ALSO OFFERS GUIDED MOUNTAIN BIKE AND CLIMBING TOURS AROUND THE CHALK CLIFFS. MUCH SMALLER BUT WORTH SEEING IS LISELUND CASTLE, WHICH HOUSES A BRANCH OF THE NATIONAL MUSEUM OF DENMARK.

IN DER UMGEBUNG. HAUPTATTRAK-TION AUF MØN SIND DIE BERÜHMTEN KREIDEKLIPPEN MØNS KLINT. WER TIEF IN DIE GEOLOGISCHE GESCHICHTE EINTAUCHEN WILL, BESUCHT DAS INTERAKTIVE NATURKUNDEMUSEUM GEOCENTER MØNS KLINT, AUCH VON PLH ARKITEKTER. HIER WERDEN GEFÜHRTE MOUNTAINBIKE- UND KLETTERTOUREN UM DIE KREIDEFEL-SEN ANGEBOTEN. VIEL KLEINER, ABER SEHENSWERT: DAS SCHLOSS LISELUND BEHERBERGT EINE AUSSENSTELLE DES DÄNISCHEN NATIONALMUSEUMS.

General view. First floor and second floor plan.
Exterior view.
Gesamtansicht. Grundriss Erdgeschoss und
Grundriss 1.Obergeschoss. Außenansicht.

Apartment with panoramic window. Terrace.
Top-down view of the surrounding area.
Wohnung mit Panoramafenster. Terrasse.
Blick auf die Umgebung von oben.

INFORMATION. ARCHITECT> ANJA RICHTER MODERSITZKI ARCHITEKTIN // 2021. HOUSE> 150 SQM // 8 GUESTS // 4 BEDROOMS // 3 BATHROOMS. ADDRESS> DORFSTRASSE 14, PANKER, GERMANY. WWW.HAUS-IN-MATZWITZ.DE

Interior view of the gallery. Living room. West view.
Haus Matzwitz from the garden.
Innenansicht Galerie. Wohnzimmer. Ansicht West.
Haus Matzwitz vom Garten.

Haus Matzwitz

PANKER, GERMANY |
DEUTSCHLAND

Located in the hinterland of the Baltic coast of Schleswig-Holstein, this wooden house is reminiscent of traditional, rural barn architecture – if it weren't for the large and asymmetrical panoramic windows. Depending on the weather, the time of day and the season, a five meter high West facing gable window is the frame for a constantly changing view. The interior and exterior lines are clear and reduced, the furnishing modern. An open-plan living room with double-height ceilings extends to the roof. Walls and ceilings are clad in light wood, and the open plan cooking and dining area is kept cozy by a wood burning stove. The external terrace extends into the volume of the house to create a sheltered external area connecting the living room with the garden.

Das Holzhaus im Hinterland der Ostseeküste Schleswig-Holsteins erinnert an klassische ländliche Scheunenarchitektur – wären da nicht die großen und asymmetrischen Panoramafenster. Das fünf Meter hohe Giebelfenster Richtung Westen bildet den Rahmen für ständig wechselnde Bilder – je nach Wetter, Tages- und Jahreszeit. Die Linienführung im Innen und Außen ist klar und reduziert, die Ausstattung modern. Der Wohnraum ist offen gestaltet, mit doppelter Raumhöhe bis unter das Dach, Wände und Decken sind mit hellem Holz bekleidet. Der offene Koch- und Essbereich wird mit einem Kaminofen besonders behaglich. Die überdachte Terrasse bildet einen geschützten Außenbereich, der das Wohnzimmer mit dem Garten verbindet

Corner seat living room. Exterior view from the terrace. Gallery. South view. Floor plans.
Sitzecke im Wohnzimmer. Außenansicht von Terrasse. Galerie. Ansicht Süd. Grundrisse.

GETTING AROUND. MATZWITZ IS LOCATED ONLY 30 MINUTES BY BIKE FROM THE HOHWACHTER BUCHT, WHERE THE BEACH AND CLIFFS ARE WORTH DISCOVERING. THE HISTORIC TOWNS IN THE VICINITY, SUCH AS EUTIN, MALENTE AND PLÖN, OFFER A VARIED CULTURAL PROGRAM, ESPECIALLY IN SUMMER.

IN DER UMGEBUNG. MATZWITZ IST NUR 30 FAHRRADMINUTEN VON DER HOHWACHTER BUCHT ENTFERNT, HIER WARTEN STRAND UND STEIL-KÜSTEN DARAUF, ENTDECKT ZU WERDEN. HISTORISCHE ORTE IN DER NAHEN UMGEBUNG, WIE Z. B. EUTIN, MALENTE UND PLÖN, BIETEN VOR ALLEM IM SOMMER EIN VIELSEITIGES KULTURPROGRAMM.

INFORMATION. INTERIOR>
AUGUST APFEL INTERIORS, SOPHIE V.
FÜRSTENBERG // 2021. 1 HOUSE,
2 APARTMENTS> 90 SQM EACH //
BACKHAUS UP TO 6 GUESTS,
MEIEREI COTTAGE UP TO 5 GUESTS
AND MEIEREI LOFT UP TO 4 GUESTS //
2 OR 3 BEDROOMS EACH //
ONE SHOWER-BATHROOM EACH.
ADDRESS> ALTE MEIEREI 1,
NEHMTEN, GERMANY.
WWW.GUT-NEHMTEN.DE

Kitchen of the Meierei cottage. A bedroom.
Exterior view Meierei Gut Nehmten.
Küche Meierei Cottage. Schlafzimmer.
Außenansicht Gut Nehmten Meierei.

Gut Nehmten

NEHMTEN, GERMANY |
DEUTSCHLAND

The Nehmten estate is located at Lake Plön, in the heart of Holstein Switzerland. The holiday homes are situated in the old dairy (Meierei) and in the bakery (Backhaus) of the property. The buildings date from around 1818 and lie right by the water. Each accommodation comes with its private garden or terrace, as well as an open fireplace. The rooms are styled individually – bright, modern and with great attention to detail. All units have access to a small beach whence it is possible to leave straight away in a canoe or SUP, practice beach yoga at sunrise or simply go for a swim. The Nehmten is a wonderful place to relax!

Gut Nehmten liegt direkt am Großen Plöner See, mitten in der Holsteinischen Schweiz. Die Feriendomizile befinden sich in der Alten Meierei und im Backhaus der Gutsanlage. Die Gebäude sind um 1818 erbaut und liegen direkt am Wasser. Jede Unterkunft hat einen eigenen Gartenplatz oder eine Terrasse sowie einen offenen Kamin. Die Räume sind individuell gestaltet – hell, modern und mit viel Liebe zum Detail. Für alle Wohneinheiten gibt es einen kleinen Strand, von dem man mit einem Kanu oder SUP direkt los fahren kann, zum Sonnenaufgang Beach-Yoga machen oder einfach nur schwimmen gehen kann. Gut Nehmten ist ein wunderbarer Ort zum Entspannen!

GETTING AROUND. BIKING, HIKING AND CANOEING TOURS AROUND AND ON THE GREAT PLÖN LAKE ARE CERTAINLY HIGHLIGHTS. IT IS ALSO POSSIBLE TO PLAY GOLF AND RIDE PONIES NEARBY. FOR THOSE WHO ARE IN THE MOOD FOR MORE ARCHITECTURE, THERE ARE CASTLES IN EUTIN, PANKER OR GETTORF OR PLACES TO VISIT IN THE HANSEATIC CITIES OF LÜBECK AND HAMBURG.

IN DER UMGEBUNG. FAHRRAD-, WANDER- UND KANUTOUREN UM UND AUF DEM GROSSEN PLÖNER SEE SIND EIN HIGHLIGHT. GOLFEN UND PONYREITEN SIND GANZ IN DER NÄHE MÖGLICH. WEM DER SINN NACH NOCH MEHR ARCHITEKTUR STEHT, DER GEHT AUF SCHLÖSSERTOUR IN EUTIN, PANKER ODER GETTORF ODER MACHT SIGHTSEEING IN DEN HANSE-STÄDTEN LÜBECK UND HAMBURG.

Exterior view Backhaus. Living room with fireplace of the Meierei cottage. Bunk in the Backhaus.
Außenansicht Backhaus. Wohnzimmer mit Kamin Meierei Cottage. Kojenzimmer Backhaus.

Interior view of the Backhaus' kitchen. Bird's eye view of Gut Nehmten. View of the Loft's living space.
Innenansicht Küche Backhaus. Vogelperspektive Gut Nehmten. Wohnraumansicht Loft.

INFORMATION. ARCHITECTS>
MÖHRING ARCHITEKTEN AND
SALTY INTERIORS // 2020.
HOUSE> 170 SQM // 6–8 GUESTS //
3 BEDROOMS // 3 BATHROOMS.
ADDRESS> SCHUBERSTRASSE 4 B,
ZINNOWITZ, GERMANY.
WWW.PANORAMAHAUSUSEDOM.DE

Kitchen and dining area. A bedroom.
Exterior view with terrace.
Küchen- und Essenbereich. Schlafzimmer.
Außenansicht mit Terrasse.

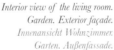

Interior view of the living room.
Garden. Exterior façade.
Innenansicht Wohnzimmer.
Garten. Außenfassade.

Panoramahaus Usedom

ZINNOWITZ, GERMANY |
DEUTSCHLAND

The Panoramahaus is a stylish place for design lovers to rest surrounded by the idyllic nature of Usedom. Modern architecture and a high-quality interior of design furniture and art make it the perfect retreat. A spacious, ground-level living room including kitchen and diningarea is characterized by its almost seamless connection to the outdoor area and the garden. Its large windows open up the view to the green garden and the wide landscape. Thus, the panoramic house convinces with its open, light-flooded interior and high-end furnishings. There are three bedrooms on the second floor, and a total of three bathrooms in the house. At its heart is the large sauna area. The focus was placed on essentials: the harmony of design, comfort and basic luxury.

Das Panoramahaus bietet Designliebhabern Erholung mit Stil, eingebettet in die idyllische Naturlandschaft Usedoms. Hier entspannt man in moderner Architektur und hochwertigem Interior aus Designmöbeln und Kunst. Der großzügige, ebenerdige Wohnraum inklusive Küche und Essbereich ist von einer fast übergangslosen Verbindung zum Außenbereich und Garten geprägt. Die großen Glasflächen leiten den Blick in das Grün des Gartens und die Weite der Landschaft. So besticht das Panoramahaus durch die offene, lichtdurchflutete Innenraumgestaltung und die hochwertige Ausstattung. Im oberen Stockwerk befinden sich drei Schlafzimmer, im Haus insgesamt drei Bäder. Das Herzstück bildet der großzügige Saunabereich, hier wurde sich auf das Wesentliche konzentriert: den Einklang von Design, Komfort und einfachem Luxus.

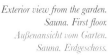

Exterior view from the garden.
Sauna. First floor.
Außenansicht vom Garten.
Sauna. Erdgeschoss.

GETTING AROUND. USEDOM COMBINES CHIC SEA RESORT ARCHITECTURE WITH UNTOUCHED NATURE IN THE PRISTINE HINTERLAND. ZINNOWITZ HAS A CHARACTERISTIC PIER AND PROMENADE AND IS ONE OF THE MOST BEAUTIFUL SPOTS OF USEDOM. ITS WIDE SANDY BEACHES ARE PERFECT FOR VACATION – FOR EITHER RELAXATION IN A BEACH CHAIR, OR ACTION ON THE SPORTS BEACH. WHEN IT RAINS, THE BERNSTEINTHERME SPA WELCOMES WITH SAUNA AND WELLNESS FACILITIES.

IN DER UMGEBUNG. USEDOM BIETET MONDÄNE BÄDERARCHITEKTUR SOWIE UNBERÜHRTE NATUR IM URSPRÜNGLICHEN HINTERLAND. DAS SEEBAD ZINNOWITZ MIT TYPISCHER SEEBRÜCKE UND PROMENADE GEHÖRT ZU DEN SCHÖNSTEN ORTEN USEDOMS. DIE BREITEN SANDSTRÄNDE SIND DIE PERFEKTE BÜHNE FÜR DEN STRANDURLAUB – OB ENTSPANNUNG IM STRANDKORB ODER ACTION AM SPORTSTRAND. BEI REGENWETTER LÄDT DIE BERNSTEINTHERME ZU SAUNA UND WELLNESS EIN.

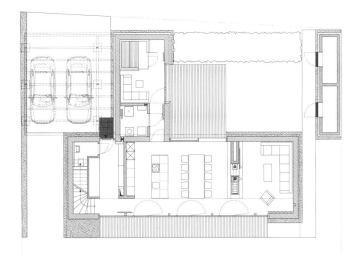

INFORMATION. ARCHITECTS>
KARL SMITH-MEYER, TOKE LARSEN,
BARBARA VON HAFFNER // 2020.
HOUSEBOAT> 16 SQM // 4 GUESTS //
1 BEDROOM // 1 BATHROOM.
ADDRESS> DANNESKIOLD-SAMSOES
ALLE 57 Z, COPENHAGEN, DENMARK.
WW.KAJHOTEL.DK

Interior view. Top view.
Exterior view from the water.
Innenansicht. Blick von oben.
Außenansicht vom Wasser.

KAJ Hotel

COPENHAGEN, DENMARK |
DÄNEMARK

KAJ Hotel is a one-room floating hotel designed as a second home, offering much more than just a hotel room. Beyond the fabulous water and harbor views, the room is equipped with a king size bed, a bathroom with shower, a full kitchenette and a balcony. The room includes a loft with two single beds in addition to the large double bed. KAJ Hotel can accommodate up to four people. It was built mainly from recycled and surplus materials. Elements with a story, wooden floors and ceilings, and the clean modern interior provide coziness dressed in modern style. Here you will enjoy the charm of a houseboat combined with Scandinavian design and the comfort of a top-class hotel.

Das KAJ Hotel ist ein schwimmendes Ein-Zimmer-Hotel, das als zweites Zuhause gedacht ist und viel mehr als nur ein Hotelzimmer bietet. Neben der fabelhaften Aussicht auf Wasser und Hafen ist das Zimmer mit einem Kingsize-Bett, Duschbad, kompletter Küchenzeile und einem Balkon ausgestattet. Zusätzlich zu dem großen Doppelbett verfügt das Zimmer über ein Loft mit zwei Einzelbetten, so dass das Hotel Platz für bis zu vier Personen bietet. Das KAJ Hotel wurde hauptsächlich aus recycelten und überschüssigen Materialien gebaut. Elemente mit Geschichte, Holzböden und -Decken und schlicht-modernes Interieur sorgen für Gemütlichkeit in modernem Gewand. Hier genießen Sie den Charme eines Hausbootes kombiniert mit skandinavischem Design und dem Komfort eines Hotels der Extraklasse.

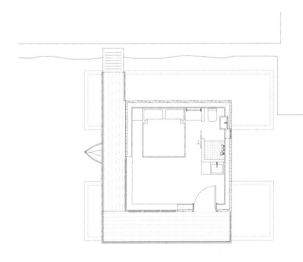

GETTING AROUND. THE NEIGHBOR-HOOD OF HOLMEN IN DOWNTOWN COPENHAGEN IS SURROUNDED BY WATER. BEYOND THE CLASSIC COPENHAGEN DESTINATIONS LIKE TIVOLI, NYHAVN, CASTLES AND MUSEUMS, THERE ARE PLENTY OF GEMS AND QUIRKY CORNERS TO DISCOVER HERE, LIKE "COPENHILL" – COPENHAGEN'S EPICENTER FOR MOUNTAIN SPORTS. SMALL CAFES AND NOMA, ONE OF THE MOST FAMOUS RESTAURANTS, ARE JUST NEXT DOOR.

IN DER UMGEBUNG. VON WAS-SER UMGEBEN LIEGT DAS VIERTEL HOLMEN IM ZENTRUM KOPENHA-GENS. NEBEN DEN KLASSISCHEN KOPENHAGEN-ZIELEN WIE TIVOLI, NYHAVN, SCHLÖSSER UND MUSEEN GIBT ES HIER JEDE MENGE KLEINO-DE UND SKURRILE ECKEN ZU ENT-DECKEN, DARUNTER „COPENHILL" – KOPENHAGENS EPIZENTRUM FÜR BERGSPORT. KLEINE CAFÉS UND EINES DER BERÜHMTESTEN RESTAURANTS, DAS NOMA, LIEGEN IN DIREKTER NACHBARSCHAFT.

Exterior view of KAJ Hotel. Floor plan.
Round window in the upper sleeping area.
Außenansicht KAJ Hotel. Grundriss.
Rundes Fenster im oberen Schlafbereich.

Interior view of the kitchen. Outdoor terrace.
Exterior view in evening mood.
Innenansicht Küche. Außenterrasse.
Außenansicht mit Abendstimmung.

INFORMATION. ARCHITECT>
SEBASTIAN KABLAU // 2011.
HOUSE> 110 SQM // 8 GUESTS //
4 BEDROOMS // 2 BATHROOMS.
ADDRESS> BASTORFER WEG 4,
OSTSEEBAD RERIK, GERMANY.
WWW.FERIENHAUS-RERIK.EU

*Exterior view of HAUS MIRO. View from the
garden at night. Interior view.
Außenansicht HAUS MIRO. Blick vom
Garten bei Nacht. Innenansicht.*

HAUS MIRO

OSTSEEBAD RERIK, GERMANY |
DEUTSCHLAND

HAUS MIRO is an exceptional vacation home, whose character is based on reduction to the essentials. The living area opens to the outside through large windows, and at the same time it connects to the top floor through a narrow staircase, thereby making it possible to experience the house's entire volume. In contrast, the bedrooms and the bathroom as rear rooms are quiet retreat areas. The small surrounding garden with several terraces and selected plants has its own intimate charm and separate areas for each apartment. The freestanding house has two apartments of 55 square meters each with two bedrooms, a shower room and an open plan cooking, dining and living area. It was built in wood structure with mainly ecological materials.

Das HAUS MIRO ist ein besonderes Ferienhaus, dessen Charakter in der Reduzierung auf das Wesentliche liegt. Der Wohnbereich öffnet sich über eine große Verglasung nach Außen und gleichzeitig verbindet er sich über die schmale Treppe mit dem Obergeschoss und macht so das gesamte Volumen des Hauses erfahrbar. Im Gegensatz dazu sind die Schlafzimmer und das Badezimmer als rückwärtige Räume ruhige Rückzugsbereiche. Der kleine, umlaufende Garten, der mit Terrassen und ausgewählter Bepflanzung seinen eigenen, intimen Charme besitzt, eröffnet jeder Wohnung einen eigenen Bereich. Das freistehende Haus umfasst zwei Wohnungen von je 55 qm mit je zwei Schlafzimmern, einem Duschbad und einem offnen Koch-, Ess- und Wohnbereich. Errichtet wurde es in Holzbaukonstrution aus vorwiegend ökologischen Materialien.

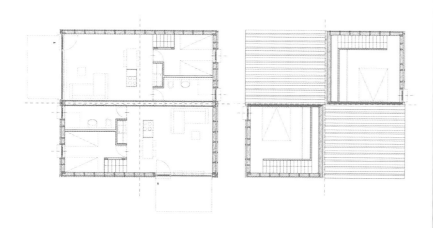

GETTING AROUND. HAUS MIRO IS LOCATED ON THE OUTSKIRTS OF THE SMALL BALTIC SEASIDE RESORT OF RERIK. THE NATURAL SANDY BEACH ALONG THE STEEP COAST CAN BE REACHED WITHIN A FEW MINUTES' WALK AND THE FINE SANDY BEACH IN THE CENTER OF THE BALTIC SEASIDE RESORT RERIK IS ALSO VERY CLOSE. DAY TRIPS TO THE BALTIC SEASIDE RESORT OF KÜHLUNGSBORN AND HEILIGENDAMM WILL TAKE YOU TO YOUR DESTINATION VIA BEAUTIFUL BIKE PATHS ALONG THE STEEP COAST.

IN DER UMGEBUNG. HAUS MIRO LIEGT AM ORTSRAND DES KLEINEN OSTSEEBADES RERIK. DER NATUR-BELASSENE SANDSTRAND MIT DER STEILKÜSTE IST IN WENIGEN MINUTEN FUSSLÄUFIG ERREICHBAR UND AUCH DER FEINE SANDSTRAND IM ZENTRUM DES OSTSEEBADS RERIK IST SCHNELL ERREICHT. TAGESTOUREN ZUM OSTSEEBAD KÜHLUNGSBORN UND HEILIGENDAMM FÜHREN SIE ÜBER WUNDERSCHÖNE RADWEGE AN DER STEILKÜSTE ZUM ZIEL.

Exterior view West. Floor plans.
Living area with terrace.
Außenansicht West. Grundrisse.
Wohnbereich mit Terrasse.

Interior view. Bedroom on the second floor.
Exterior view South.
Innenansicht. Schlafzimmer im Obergeschoss.
Außenansicht Süd.

INFORMATION. ARCHITECT>
CARSTEN OTTO // LANDSCAPE
ARCHITECT> SABINE OTTO // 2018.
HOUSES> HAUS LÜTT MARTEN
55 SQM AND HAUS SÖT MINE
75 SQM // 4–6 GUESTS //
2–3 BEDROOMS // 1–2 BATHROOMS.
ADDRESS> TEUFELSBERG 6 A,
STUBBENFELDE, GERMANY.
WWW.SEEHAEUSER-USEDOM.DE

Interior view dining area. Sleeping area.
Vacation homes from below.
Innenansicht Essbereich. Schlafbereich.
Ferienhäuser von unten.

Seehäuser Usedom

STUBBENFELDE, GERMANY | DEUTSCHLAND

These vacation homes represent modern architecture combined with ecological construction; they are made entirely of glulam timber elements. Warm material wood also determines the interior design of the rooms. Guests feel the atmosphere to be quaint, warm and cozy at once – as well as modern, easy and flooded with light. Both rental houses, Söt Mine and Lütt Marten, are equipped with a sauna and a fireplace. The houses have an atmosphere of relaxed lightness because of their puristic structure as well as carefully selected and harmoniously arranged interior furnishings, featuring a perfect mix of natural elegance, Scandinavian design, and modern coziness. The proximity to the beach and the surrounding nature ensure a carefree vacation.

Die Ferienhäuser stehen für die Verbindung von moderner Architektur und ökologischer Bauweise, sie sind komplett aus Brettschichtholzelementen errichtet. Auch im Inneren bestimmt das warme Material Holz die Gestaltung der Räume. Gäste erleben die Atmosphäre zugleich als urig, warm und gemütlich – wie auch modern, leicht und lichtdurchflutet. Beide zur Vermietung stehende Häuser, Söt Mine und Lütt Marten, sind mit Sauna und Kamin ausgestattet. Mit einer gelungenen Kombination aus naturbelassener Eleganz, skandinavischem Design und moderner Gemütlichkeit strahlen die Häuser aufgrund ihrer puristischen Bauweise und der liebevoll ausgesuchten sowie aufeinander abgestimmten Inneneinrichtung eine entspannte Leichtigkeit aus. Die Nähe zum Strand und zur umliegenden Natur macht den Urlaub unbeschwert.

Front view. View from the hallway.
Vorderansicht. Blick von Flur.

Bedroom. Interior view.
Side view. Floor plans.
Schlafzimmer. Innenansicht.
Seitenansicht. Grundrisse.

GETTING AROUND. ON ONE SIDE THERE IS THE PICTURESQUE KÖLPINSEE, ON THE OTHER SIDE, JUST BEHIND THE TREES, THE BEACH OF THE BALTIC SEA – THE PROXIMITY TO THE WATER IS AN INVITATION TO GO FOR A WALK OR TO DO SOME SPORTS! THE BEACH OF STUBBENFELDE IS NOT AS CROWDED AS THE BEACHES OF THE BIG BALTIC RESORTS, EVEN IN HIGH SUMMER, AND IT IS QUITE NORMAL TO SPOT SOME AMBER STONES.

IN DER UMGEBUNG. AUF DER EINEN SEITE DER MALERISCHE KÖLPINSEE, AUF DER ANDEREN SEITE GLEICH HINTER DEN BÄUMEN DER OSTSEE-STRAND – DIE WASSERNÄHE LÄDT ZU SPAZIERGÄNGEN UND SPORTLICHER AKTIVITÄT EIN! DER STRAND VON STUBBENFELDE IST AUCH IM HOCHSOMMER NICHT SO ÜBERLAUFEN WIE DIE STRÄNDE DER GROSSEN OST-SEEBÄDER UND ES LASSEN SICH HIER REGELMÄSSIG BERNSTEINE FINDEN.

INFORMATION. ARCHITECTS>
VIPP AND STUDIO DAVID THULSTRUP
// INTERIOR DESIGN> JULIE CLOOS
MØLSGAARD // 2019.
HOUSE> 200 SQM // 4 GUESTS //
2 BEDROOMS // 2 BATHROOMS.
ADDRESS> STRANDØRE 5,
COPENHAGEN ØSTERBRO, DENMARK.
WWW.VIPP.COM/EN/HOTEL/VIPP-
CHIMNEY-HOUSE

The Vipp Chimney House living room.
Interior of kitchen area. Exterior view.
Wohnzimmer Vipp Chimney House.
Innenansicht Küchenbereich. Außenansicht.

Vipp Chimney House

COPENHAGEN ØSTERBRO,
DENMARK | DÄNEMARK

The Vipp Chimney House is a former water pumping station built in 1902 with a remarkable 35-meter chimney. When converting it into a 200-square-meter guest house, great care was taken to preserve the historic façade. The original industrial space was expanded with state-of-the-art cladding and furnished with Vipp products and selected artwork. The ceiling of the atrium is 8.5 meters high and provides a view of the old chimney through a skylight. Arched steel-framed glass doors, custom terrazzo floors, a modern steel staircase and open access to a private terrace are some of the architectural highlights. Two bathrooms, two bedrooms and a large open kitchen, dining and living area invite guests to linger.

Das Vipp Chimney House ist ein umgebautes, ehemaliges Wasserpumpwerk aus dem Jahr 1902 mit einem bemerkenswerten, 35 Meter hohen Schornstein. Bei der Umnutzung zum 200 qm großen Gästehaus wurde viel Wert auf den Erhalt der historischen Fassade gelegt. Der ursprüngliche Industrieraum wurde mit einem modernen Overlay erweitert und mit Vipp-Produkten und kuratierten Kunstwerken ausgestattet. Im Atrium beträgt die Deckenhöhe 8,5 m und gibt den Blick durch ein Oberlicht auf den alten Schornstein frei. Rundbogentüren aus stahlgerahmtem Glas, maßgeschneiderte Terrazzoböden, eine moderne Stahltreppe und ein offener Zugang zur privaten Terrasse sind einige der architektonischen Highlights. Zwei Bäder, zwei Schlafzimmer und ein großer, offener Küchen-, Ess- und Wohnbereich laden die Gäste zum verweilen ein.

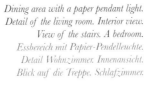

Dining area with a paper pendant light.
Detail of the living room. Interior view.
View of the stairs. A bedroom.
Essbereich mit Papier-Pendelleuchte.
Detail Wohnzimmer. Innenansicht.
Blick auf die Treppe. Schlafzimmer.

GETTING AROUND. LOCATED ONLY 10 MINUTES FROM THE HEART OF COPENHAGEN IN THE DISTRICT OF ØSTERBRO, THE CITY CAN BE EASILY EXPLORED ON FOOT. THE BEACH SVANEMØLLEN IS A GREAT PLACE TO SWIM AND THE PROMENADES ALONG THE COAST BETWEEN COPENHAGEN NORDHAVN AND TUBORG HAVN IN HELLERUP ARE NEARBY.

IN DER UMGEBUNG. NUR 10 MINUTEN VOM HERZEN KOPENHAGENS ENTFERNT IM STADTTEIL ØSTERBRO GELEGEN LÄSST SICH DIE STADT BEQUEM ZU FUSS ERKUNDEN. DER STRAND SVANEMØLLEN LÄDT ZUM BADEN EIN UND DIE STRANDPROMENADEN, DIE SICH ENTLANG DER KÜSTE ZWISCHEN DEM KOPENHAGENER STADTTEIL NORDHAVN UND TUBORG HAVN IN HELLERUP ENTDECKEN, LIEGEN IN DIREKTER NÄHE.

INFORMATION. ARCHITECTS>
KLM-ARCHITEKTEN UND INGENIEURE
GMBH // ARCHITECTS LPH 5–8>
HATZIUS SARRAMONA ARCHITEKTEN
// 2017. LODGES AND APARTMENTS>
FROM 48 TO 200 SQM PER LODGE //
KLEINE PERLE 2 GUESTS, GROSSES
GLÜCK 4 + 4 GUESTS, HOCH HINAUS 4
+ 6 GUESTS, ABENDROT 4 + 4 GUESTS,
KLEEGRÜN 2 GUESTS, HIMMELBLAU 2
+ 1 GUESTS, GOLDGELB 2 + 2 GUESTS
// 1 TO 3 BEDROOMS EACH // 1 TO 3
BATHROOMS EACH.
ADDRESS> SCHWENNAUSTRASSE 37,
GLÜCKSBURG, GERMANY.
WWW.GLUECK-IN-SICHT.DE

Hoch Hinaus living room.
Hoch Hinaus by the cliffs.
Wohnzimmer Hoch Hinaus.
Hoch Hinaus an der Steilküste.

Glück in Sicht Ostseelodges

GLÜCKSBURG, GERMANY |
DEUTSCHLAND

Vacation homes of various sizes are carefully positioned in the park-like setting, with sweeping views of the forest and coastal landscape. Each house is characterized by Nordic unobtrusiveness and elegant simplicity, from the architecture to the furnishings. The dark façade contrasts with the light-flooded interiors. The houses' hub is a living and dining area combined with an open kitchen and large dining table. A sauna, an electric fireplace, and a multimedia equipment make the accommodations a cozy place even on colder days. Indoor and outdoor spaces are connected by the open design, generous window fronts to the terraces open the view to water, forest, and meadow as well as the coast of Denmark.

Ferienhäuser unterschiedlicher Größe sind in der parkartigen Umgebung sorgfältig positioniert, wobei sich weitläufige Ausblicke in die Wald- und Küstenlandschaft eröffnen. Nordische Zurückhaltung und elegante Schlichtheit prägen jedes Haus von der Architektur bis zur Einrichtung. Die dunkle Fassade steht im Kontrast zu den lichtdurchfluteten Innenräumen. Mittelpunkt der Häuser ist ein kombinierter Wohn- und Essbereich mit offener Küche und großem Esstisch. Sauna, elektrischer Kamin und multimediale Ausstattung machen die Unterkünfte auch an kälteren Tagen zu einem gemütlichen Ort. Innen- und Außenräume werden durch die offene Bauweise miteinander verbunden, großzügige Fensterfronten mit vorgelagerten Terrassen öffnen den Blick auf Wasser, Wald und Wiese sowie die Küste von Dänemark.

Evening mood Großes Glück.
Family bedroom.
Abendstimmung Großes Glück.
Familienschlafzimmer.

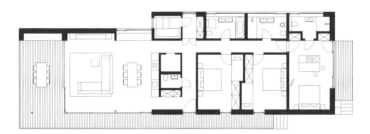

GETTING AROUND. GLÜCKSBURG IS KNOWN FOR ITS BEAUTIFUL, MOATED CASTLE, THE ROSARIUM, THE THERMAL SPA FÖRDELAND-THERME AND THE PENINSULA HOLNIS. THE FLENSBURG FJORD WITH ITS NATURAL BEACHES IS WAITING TO BE EXPLORED. THE HARBOR CITY OF FLENSBURG IS CLOSE TO GLÜCKS-BURG. FOR DANISH DESIGN, HEAD TO THE TOWN OF SONDERBURG, WHICH CAN BE REACHED BY FERRY.

IN DER UMGEBUNG. GLÜCKSBURG IST BEKANNT FÜR SEIN WUNDER-SCHÖNES WASSERSCHLOSS, DAS ROSARIUM, DIE FÖRDELANDTHERME UND DIE HALBINSEL HOLNIS. DIE FLENSBURGER FÖRDE MIT DEN NA-TURBELASSENEN STRÄNDEN WARTET DARAUF ERKUNDET ZU WERDEN. DIE HAFENSTADT FLENSBURG LIEGT IN UNMITTELBARER NÄHE ZU GLÜCKS-BURG. DÄNISCHES DESIGN FINDET MAN IN DER STADT SONDERBURG, DIE MAN MIT DER FÄHRE ERREICHT.

Großes Glück Küstenflair living room. Floor plans.
Exterior view Kleine Perle.
Großes Glück Küstenflair Wohnraum. Grundrisse.
Außenansicht Kleine Perle.

Großes Glück Küstenflair. Interior view Kleine Perle.
Hoch Hinaus cooking and living area.
Großes Glück Küstenflair. Innenansicht Kleine Perle.
Kochen- und Wohnbereich Hoch Hinaus.

INFORMATION. ARCHITECTS>
BEISSERT + GRUSS ARCHITEKTEN BDA
// 2020. HOUSES> CA. 2,500 SQM //
26 GUESTS // 11 BEDROOMS //
8 BATHROOMS.
ADDRESS> ALLEE 4, ALTENKREMPE,
GERMANY.
WWW.HASSELBURG.DE

North-West exterior view. Interior view of the hall.
Dining area.
Außenansicht Nord-West. Innenansicht Saal.
Koch- und Essbereich.

Kuhhaus Gut Hasselburg

ALTENKREMPE, GERMANY |
DEUTSCHLAND

After the conversion and renovation of the thatched barn, the sheep barn and the gatehouse of Hasselburg Manor, the South barn (former cow house) was the last part of the baroque building complex to undergo comprehensive renovation and conversion. Built around 1760 and listed as a historic monument, the barn was converted into a concert hall and guest house. Apartments, guest rooms and seminar rooms make the South barn complete. On the one hand they meet the high demand for the Hasselburg manor as a place of recreation and on the other hand they give artists the space to settle down for the duration of a project. Guests can enjoy the cultural environment in beautiful individually designed vacation homes, furnished with natural materials.

Nach den Umbauten und Sanierungen der reetgedeckten Scheune, des Schafstalls und des Torhauses Gut Hasselburg wurde die Südscheune (ehemaliges Kuhhaus) als letztes Gebäude des barocken Bauhofgefüges einer umfassenden Sanierung und Umnutzung unterzogen. Das um 1760 entstandene und denkmalgeschützte Stallgebäude wurde in ein Konzert- und Gästehaus umgewandelt. Komplettiert wird die Südscheune durch Ferienwohnungen, Gästezimmer und Seminarräume, die einerseits der hohen Nachfrage nach dem Erholungsort Gut Hasselburg gerecht werden, andererseits Künstlern den Raum bieten, sich für die Dauer eines Projektes niederzulassen. Als Feriengast geniesst man in hochwertig gestalteten, mit natürlichen Materialien ausgestatteten Ferienwohnungen die kulturelle Umgebung.

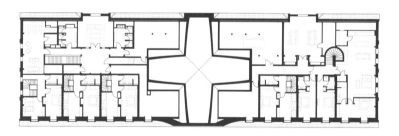

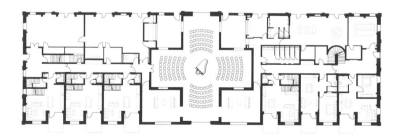

GETTING AROUND. BEYOND THE ARCHITECTURE TO BE DISCOVERED, GUT HASSELBURG OFFERS A LOT OF CULTURAL EVENTS SUCH AS CONCERTS (E.G. THE SCHLESWIG-HOLSTEIN MUSIC FESTIVAL), READINGS AND EVENTS FOR CHILDREN. THE BALTIC SEA COAST CAN BE REACHED IN A VERY SHORT TIME, AND THERE ARE ALSO MANY RURAL ESTATES, WIDE FIELDS, AND BEAUTIFUL NATURE TO DISCOVER.

IN DER UMGEBUNG. NEBEN DER ARCHITEKTUR, DIE ES HIER ZU ENT-DECKEN GIBT, BIETET DAS GUT HASSELBURG ZAHLREICHE KULTUR-VERANSTALTUNGEN WIE KONZERTE (Z. B. DAS SCHLESWIG-HOLSTEIN MUSIK FESTIVAL), LESUNGEN UND VERANSTALTUNGEN FÜR KINDER. DIE OSTSEEKÜSTE IST SCHNELL ERREICHT, AUSSERDEM LADEN ZAHLREICHE LANDGÜTER, WEITE FELDER UND DIE SCHÖNE NATUR ZU AUSFLÜGEN EIN.

South-East exterior view. Floor plans.
Interior view of the hall.
Außenansicht Süd-Ost. Grundrisse.
Innenansicht Saal.

A bedroom. Interior view.
Exterior view of an apartment with terrace.
Schlafzimmer. Innenansicht.
Außenansicht einzelne Wohnung mit Terrasse.

INFORMATION. ARCHITECT>
KRAUSE SCHRECK PARTNERSCHAFT //
2018. BOUTIQUE HOTEL> 720 SQM //
24 GUESTS // 10 BEDROOMS //
11 BATHROOMS.
ADDRESS> FISCHERGRUBE 83,
LÜBECK, GERMANY.
WWW.FISHERSLOFT-HOTEL.DE

Sleeping area. Interior view from above.
Living area with fireplace.
Schlafbereich. Innenansicht von oben.
Wohnbereich mit Kamin.

Kitchen and dining area. Interior view of a room.
Küchen- und Essbereich. Innenansicht Zimmer.

Hotel Fisher's Loft

LÜBECK, GERMANY |
DEUTSCHLAND

Fisher's Loft boutique hotel welcomes its guests in a 250-year-old rococo warehouse typical of the Hanseatic city. This listed building provides the perfect setting for an authentic experience of Lübeck's architectural culture. The 10 rooms of the hotel Garni are characterized by discreet colors, wood, and steel. There are three categories of rooms ranging from 35 to 65 square meters, some of which are on two levels. They all share modern, timeless comfort in terms of furnishings and fittings. This comes from the skillfully designed lighting, historic beams and brickwork; contemporary furniture and top-quality materials used for the interior, such as custom-made linen bedding. The privately managed hotel combines past and present to perfection!

Das Boutiquehotel Fisher's Loft empfängt seine Gäste in einem hansestadttypischen, 250 Jahre alten Rokoko Speicher. In dem denkmalgeschützten Gebäude erlebt man authentisch die besondere Baukultur Lübecks. Zurückhaltend eingesetzte Farben, Holz und Stahl prägen die Räume der zehn Zimmer des Garni-Hotels. Drei Zimmerkategorien von 35 bis 65 qm – teilweise über zwei Ebenen – stehen zur Verfügung. Allen gemeinsam ist die moderne, zeitlose Gemütlichkeit von Einrichtung und Ausstattung. Dafür sorgen die gekonnt geplante Beleuchtung, historische Balken und Mauerwerk, die moderne Möblierung und die hochwertigen Materialien der Ausstattung, wie zum Beispiel die eigens gefertigte Leinenbettwäsche. Historie und Heute werden in dem privat geführten Hotel auf das Beste vereint!

Exterior view from the street. A bedroom.
En-suite bathroom. Dining area.
Außenansicht von der Straße. Schlafzimmer.
En-suite Badezimmer. Essbereich.

GETTING AROUND. RIGHT IN THE HISTORIC OLD TOWN, VISITORS CAN FOLLOW IN THE FOOTSTEPS OF THE BUDDENBROOKS OR GÜNTER GRASS. HISTORY IS ALIVE AMONG THE HISTORIC WAREHOUSES AND THE NUMEROUS MUSEUMS (BEHNHAUS, HANSEMUSEUM, ST. ANNEN). THE BEACHES OF THE LÜBECK BAY ARE ONLY 20 KILOMETERS AWAY AND ARE WORTH A TRIP TO THE COAST, ESPECIALLY IN SUMMER!

IN DER UMGEBUNG. DIREKT IN DER HISTORISCHEN ALTSTADT GELEGEN WANDELT MAN AUF DEN SPUREN DER BUDDENBROOKS ODER GÜNTER GRASS. ZWISCHEN HISTORISCHEN SPEICHERN UND DEN ZAHLREICHEN MUSEEN (BEHNHAUS, HANSEMUSEUM, ST. ANNEN) WIRD GESCHICHTE LE-BENDIG. DIE STRÄNDE DER LÜBECKER BUCHT SIND NUR 20 KM ENTFERNT UND BESONDERS IM SOMMER EINEN AUSFLUG AN DIE KÜSTE WERT!

INFORMATION. ARCHITECT>
SIGURD LARSEN // 2019. 3 CABINS>
31 SQM + 20 SQM ROOF TERRACE //
2 GUESTS PER CABIN // 1 BEDROOM //
1 BATHROOM.
ADDRESS> ALS ODDE, DENMARK.
WWW.LOVTAG.DK

View from below. Interior of the living area.
The cottage in midst of nature.
Blick von unten. Innenansicht Wohnbereich.
Die Hütte inmitten der Natur.

Treetop Hotel Løvtag

ALS ODDE, DENMARK |
DENMARK

In a small, picturesque forest there are three extraordinary tree houses floating between the treetops of deciduous and coniferous trees. These tree houses can accommodate up to four overnight guests, are furnished in a modern and puristic style and are equipped with a kitchen, bathroom, and bedroom. An outdoor shower is installed on the cabin's front. The treetop lodges enclose a tree; the trunk literally grows through the house. The access to the roof top terrace gives the impression that you continue to "climb" the tree to reach the treetop. There are fantastic views of the forest in all directions from up here and through the panoramic windows.

In einem kleinen, malerischen Wald schweben drei besondere Baumhäuser zwischen den Wipfeln von Laub- und Nadelbäumen. Die Baumhäuser bieten Platz für bis zu vier Schlafgäste, sind modern und puristisch möbliert und mit Küche, Bad und Schlafzimmer ausgestattet. An der Fassade der Hütte ist eine Außendusche angebracht. Die Baumkronenhütten umschließen einen Baum, der Stamm wächst quasi durch das Haus hindurch. Der Zugang zur Dachterrasse vermittelt den Eindruck, dass man den Baum weiter „erklimmt", um die Baumkrone zu erreichen. Von hier aus und auch durch die Panoramafenster bieten sich phantastische Ausblicke auf den Wald in alle Richtungen.

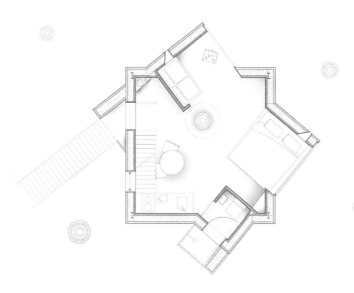

GETTING AROUND. NEARBY, MARIAGER FJORD IS THE LONGEST FJORD IN DENMARK AND OFFERS THE BEST OPPORTUNITIES FOR FISHING, KAYAKING, OR CYCLING AND HIKING ALONG THE SHORES. FROM A CULINARY POINT OF VIEW, A VISIT TO THE TRADITIONAL RESTAURANT ALS KRO OR A LOCAL WINETASTING AT THE SMALL ODDE KYSTVINERI WINERY IS RECOMMENDED.

IN DER UMGEBUNG. DER NAHEGE-LEGENE MARIAGER FJORD IST DER LÄNGSTE FJORD DÄNEMARKS UND BIETET BESTE MÖGLICHKEITEN ZUM ANGELN, KAJAKFAHREN ODER RAD- UND WANDERTOUREN ENTLANG DER UFER. KULINARISCH EMPFIEHLT SICH EIN BESUCH DES HISTORISCHEN GASTHAUSES ALS KRO ODER EINE KOSTPROBE DES ÖRTLICHEN WEINS IN DER KLEINEN WEINKELLEREI ODDE KYSTVINERI.

Sleeping area with panoramic window.
Floor plan. Outdoor terrace.
Schlafbereich mit Panoramafenster.
Grundriss. Außenterrasse.

The cabin from below. Interior view.
Exterior view of the cabin.
Hütte von unten. Innenansicht.
Außenansicht der Hütte.

INFORMATION. ARCHITECTS> TOBIAS RUGE, RUGE GÖLLNER // 2015. HOUSES> CA. 120 SQM // 4 GUESTS // 2 BEDROOMS // 2 BATHROOMS. ADDRESS> SCHWEDENSCHANZE 2–2A, DIERHAGEN, GERMANY. WWW.AUFSFISCHLAND.DE WWW.SIEGFRIED-AM-STRAND.DE

Dining area. Interior view.
Essbereich. Innenansicht.

Ferienhäuser Trudel + Siegfried

DIERHAGEN, GERMANY |
DEUTSCHLAND

It is by their quiet location, simple beauty and functionality that the two modern wooden cottages are so captivating. The bright and natural ambience results from contemporary, open plan architecture. The naturally grayed larch wood façade contrasts with the white interiors featuring solid oak parquet flooring and select color accents. The spacious living and dining area with a high-quality equipped kitchen and a fireplace is the heart of the house. Large sliding windows open the view to the Saaler Bodden lagoon and connect the first floor with the garden. Sunny and shady spots are available on the east and west terraces at any time of the day. On the upper floor there are two spacious bedrooms with double bed and a bathroom with shower and double vanity.

Die zwei modernen Holzhäuser bestechen durch ihre ruhige Lage, schlichte Schönheit und Funktionalität. Die moderne, offene Architektur schafft ein lichtdurchflutetes und naturverbundenes Ambiente. Im Kontrast zur natürlich vergrauten Lärchenholzfassade stehen die weißen Innenräume mit ihrem massiven Eichenholzparkett und den ausgesuchten Farbakzenten. Der großzügige Wohn- und Essbereich mit hochwertig ausgestatteter Küche und Kaminofen ist das Herzstück des Hauses. Große Schiebefenster geben den Ausblick bis zum Saaler Bodden frei und öffnen das Erdgeschoss zum Garten. Hier bieten Ost- und Westterrasse Sonnen- und Schattenplätze zu jeder Tageszeit. Im Obergeschoss befinden sich zwei geräumige Schlafzimmer mit Doppelbett und ein Badezimmer mit Dusche und Doppelwaschtisch.

Exterior view from the garden.
Interior view of the kitchen.
Außenansicht vom Garten.
Innenansicht Küche.

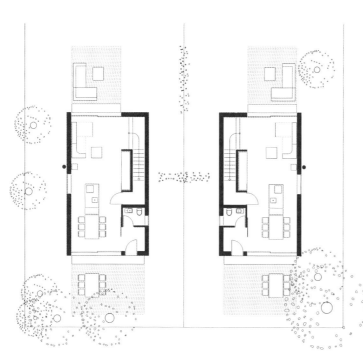

GETTING AROUND. THE WIDE SANDY BEACH IS ONLY 200 METERS AWAY, THE BALTIC SEA AND THE BODDEN LAGOON OFFER THE BEST CONDITIONS FOR SAILING, SURFING, KITING OR STAND UP PADDLING – AND THOSE INTERESTED IN CULTURE INSTEAD OF SPORTS HAVE PLENTY DESTINATIONS NEARBY, NAMELY THE HANSEATIC CITIES OF WISMAR, ROSTOCK AND STRALSUND OR THE ARTISTS' VILLAGE OF AHRENSHOOP WITH ITS GALLERIES AND CAFÉS.

IN DER UMGEBUNG. DER BREITE SANDSTRAND LIEGT NUR 200 METER ENTFERNT, OSTSEE UND BODDEN BIETEN DIE BESTEN VORAUSSETZUNGEN ZUM SEGELN, SURFEN, KITEN ODER STAND UP PADDELING – UND WER KULTUR STATT SPORT SUCHT, HAT MIT DEN HANSESTÄDTEN WISMAR, ROSTOCK UND STRALSUND ODER DEM KÜNSTLERDORF AHRENSHOOP MIT SEINEN GALERIEN UND CAFÉS VIELE AUSFLUGSZIELE IN DER NÄHE.

INFORMATION. ARCHITECTS>
MÖHRING ARCHITEKTEN // WIECK9
2018 AND WIECK11 2021.
2 HOUSES> 178 SQM EACH //
6 GUESTS EACH // 3 BEDROOMS
EACH // 2 BATHROOMS EACH.
ADDRESS> BLIESENRADER WEG 9
AND 11, WIECK, GERMANY.
WWW.QUARTIER-WIECK.DE

Kitchen and dining area. Interior view.
View from the garden.
Küchen- und Essbereich. Innenansicht.
Blick vom Garten.

Quartier-Wieck

WIECK, GERMANY |
DEUTSCHLAND

Quartier-Wieck holiday homes consist of the two houses WIECK9 and WIECK11 and is located on the Darss peninsula, only 300 meters from the Bodtstedter Bodden lagoon. Light is its architectural protagonist. Featuring a large skylight and floor-to-ceiling windows in the central kitchen, the house is bathed in light. Ingenious black wood cladding with vertical, overlapping panels generate the interplay of light and shadow. The surfaces throughout the house are characterized by aesthetic breaks resulting from the mix of exquisite materials such as shell limestone, oak wood, sawn larch wood, copper and stainless steel. The two houses have the same floor plan but differ in the design of the interior. Both feature contemporary artwork from the owners' private collection.

Das Ferienhausensemble Quartier-Wieck mit den beiden Häusern WIECK9 und WIECK11 liegt auf dem Darß, nur 300 Meter vom Bodtstedter Bodden entfernt. Architektonischer Hauptakteur ist das Licht. Ein großes Oberlicht und bodentiefe Fensterfronten in der zentralen Küche sorgen für eine strahlende Helligkeit im Haus. Die raffinierte, schwarze Holzfassade mit vertikaler, überlappender Verlegung sorgt für ein Spiel von Licht und Schatten. Die hochwertige Materialauswahl ergibt Oberflächen voller Sprünge: Muschelkalk, Eichenholz, sägeraues Lärchenholz, Kupferdach und eine Arbeitsplatte aus Edelstahl. Die beiden Häuser haben den gleichen Grundriss, unterscheiden sich aber im Design des Innenraumes. In beiden werden zeitgenössische Kunstwerke aus der privaten Sammlung der Eigentümer gezeigt.

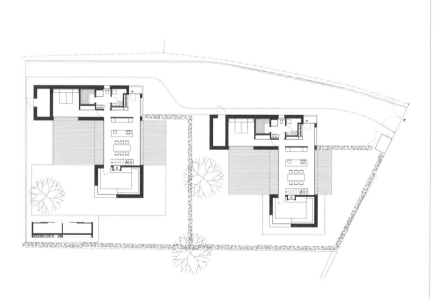

GETTING AROUND. THE VILLAGE OF WIECK IS THE PERFECT DEPARTURE POINT FOR TRIPS TO NATURE: THE BEACH EXTENDING FROM AHRENSHOOP TO PREROW IS UNIQUE. JUST LIKE THE DARSS FOREST, IT BELONGS TO THE NATIONAL PARK VORPOMMERSCHE BODDENLAND-SCHAFT. THERE ARE OVER THIRTY HIKING AND CYCLING TRAILS THROUGH THE FOREST. THE WIND, WHICH IS ALMOST ALWAYS PRESENT, MAKES THE BODDEN LAGOON AN IDEAL SURFING AND KITING SPOT.

IN DER UMGEBUNG. DER ORT WIECK IST IDEALER AUSGANGSPUNKT FÜR AUSFLÜGE IN DIE NATUR: DER STRAND VON AHRENSHOOP BIS PREROW BEEINDRUCKT AUF EINZIGARTIGE WEISE. ER GEHÖRT WIE DER DARSSER WALD ZUM NATIONALPARK VORPOM-MERSCHE BODDENLANDSCHAFT. AUF UNZÄHLIGEN WEGEN KANN DER WALD DURCHWANDERT ODER MIT DEM RAD DURCHQUERT WERDEN. DER FAST IMMER VORHANDENE WIND MACHT DEN BODDEN ZUM IDEALEN SURF- UND KITEREVIER.

INFORMATION. ARCHITECT>
MISSFELDT KRASS // INTERIOR
DESIGN> MOODWORKS // 2021.
HOLIDAY HOME> 394 SQM //
14 GUESTS + 2 CHILDREN //
5 BEDROOMS // 3 BATHROOMS
+ 2 GUEST WCS.
ADDRESS> SCHLAGSDORF 19,
FEHMARN, GERMANY.
WWW.LANDLOFT27.DE

Interior view bedroom. Kitchen.
Exterior view from garden.
Innenansicht Schlafzimmer. Küche.
Außenansicht vom Garten.

Dining area with fireplace.
Landloft27 exterior view.
Essbereich mit Kamin.
Außenfassade Landloft27.

Landloft27

FEHMARN, GERMANY |
DEUTSCHLAND

Stylish. Rustic. Individual. Perfect for active vacations with friends or the whole family. The vacation home offers plenty of space for up to 14 people and two small children. Peace, relaxation, and wellness in an idyllic location – and the Baltic Sea close by. The Landloft27 is modern and furnished with attention to detail. Its spaciousness and beautiful views are captivating. There is direct access to the terrace and garden from the separate sauna house with relaxation room and Swedish stove. The fenced garden with plenty of seating, boules court, old trees, newly planted fruit trees and the typical Fehmarn hedges offers many opportunities for retreat. A small snack garden and the fruit trees invite to harvest.

Stilvoll. Ländlich. Persönlich. Perfekt für Aktivurlaub mit Freunden oder der ganzen Familie. Das Ferienhaus bietet viel Platz für bis zu 14 Personen und zwei Kleinkinder. Ruhe, Entspannung und Wellness in idyllischer Lage – und die Ostsee ganz in der Nähe. Das Landloft27 ist modern und mit Liebe zum Detail eingerichtet. Es besticht durch Großzügigkeit und schöne Aussichten. Vom separaten Saunahaus mit Ruheraum und Schwedenofen hat man direkten Zugang zu Terrasse und Garten. Der eingezäunte Garten mit reichlich Sitzgelegenheiten, Boulebahn, altem Baumbestand, neu gepflanzten Obstbäumen und typisch fehmarnschen Knicks bietet viele Rückzugsmöglichkeiten. Ein kleiner Naschgarten und die Obstbäume laden zur Ernte ein.

Living room. Attic area. Sauna.
Alcoves and windows with seats in the attic.
Floor plans first floor and second floor.
Wohnzimmer. Spitzboden. Sauna.
Alkoven und Sitzfenster in Spitzboden.
Grundrisse Erdgeschoss und 1. Obergeschoss.

GETTING AROUND. A BEACH FOR SWIMMING CAN BE REACHED WITHIN TEN MINUTES BY BIKE. FEHMARN IS PERFECT FOR WATER SPORTS LIKE SURFING, KITING, STAND-UP PADDLING, WATER SKIING, WAKE-BOARDING, AND FISHING. THERE ARE 300 KILOMETERS OF CYCLING OR HIKING TRAILS ON THE ISLAND, RIGHT ON THE DIKE OR ACROSS THE VILLAGES, AND WITH STOP-OVERS AT A BEACH BAR OR FARM CAFÉ.

IN DER UMGEBUNG. EIN BA-DESTRAND KANN IN NUR ZEHN MINUTEN MIT DEM RAD ERREICHT WERDEN. FEHMARN IST PERFEKT FÜR WASSERSPORT WIE SURFEN, KITEN, STAND-UP-PADDELN, WASSERSKIFAH-REN, WAKEBOARDEN UND ANGELN GEEIGNET. AUF DER INSEL GIBT ES 300 KM RAD- BZW. WANDERWEGE, DIREKT AUF DEM DEICH ODER ÜBER DIE DÖRFER MIT EINEM ZWISCHEN-STOPP AN EINER STRANDBAR ODER AN EINEM HOFCAFÉ.

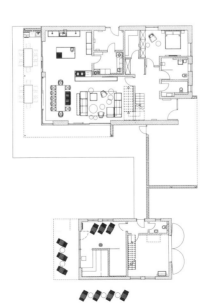

INFORMATION. ARCHITECT>
CAMILLA BJØRNVAD // 2017–2021.
HOTEL> 2,500 SQM // 118 GUESTS //
61 BEDROOMS // 61 BATHROOMS.
ADDRESS> H. C. ANDERSENS BLVD. 8,
COPENHAGEN, DENMARK.
WWW.HOTELALEXANDRA.DK

The 50s room. Front of the hotel.
The Panton suite.
Das 50er-Jahre-Zimmer. Hotelfassade.
Panton-Suite.

Hotel Alexandra

COPENHAGEN, DENMARK |
DÄNEMARK

It's like staying with a Danish design loving friend in Copenhagen! Alexandra boutique hotel has gathered a unique and large collection of Danish mid-century furniture. As a special tribute to the world famous Danish designers Hans J. Wegner, Bodil Kjær, Kai Kristiansen, Ole Wanscher, Børge Mogensen, Arne Jacobsen, Verner Panton, Nanna Ditzel, Finn Juhl and many others, all rooms and the lobby are furnished with the most beautiful Danish mid-century furniture. A very special place rich in design enthusiasm for the 50's and 60's.

Wie ein Aufenthalt bei einem dänischen Designliebhaber Freund in Kopenhagen! Das Boutiquehotel Alexandra hat eine einzigartige und große Sammlung von dänischen Möbeln aus der Mitte des Jahrhunderts zusammengetragen. Als besondere Hommage an die weltberühmten dänischen Designer Hans J. Wegner, Bodil Kjær, Kai Kristiansen, Ole Wanscher, Borge Mogensen, Arne Jacobsen, Verner Panton, Nanna Ditzel, Finn Juhl und viele andere, sind alle Zimmer und die Lobby mit den schönsten dänischen Mid-Century-Möbeln ausgestattet. Ein ganz besonderer Ort mit Designbegeisterung für die 50er und 60er-Jahren.

GETTING AROUND. LOCATED IN THE CENTER OF COPENHAGEN – JUST AROUND THE CORNER FROM CITY HALL SQUARE, THE LATIN QUARTER, THE MAIN SHOPPING AREA AND TIVOLI GARDENS – THIS IS A GREAT PLACE FOR WALKING AROUND OR RIDING A BIKE. THERE ARE 300 METERS TO CLIMB TO THE TOP OF THE RUNDETÅRN – THE VIEW OVER THE CITY COMPENSATES FOR EVERY EFFORT!

IN DER UMGEBUNG. IM ZENTRUM KOPENHAGENS GELEGEN – GLEICH UM DIE ECKE VOM RATHAUSPLATZ, DEM LATEINISCHEN VIERTEL, DEM HAUPTEINKAUFSVIERTEL UND DEM TIVOLI-GARTEN – BIETEN SICH HIER AUSFÜHRLICHE BUMMEL ZU FUSS ODER PER RAD AN. 300 METER MÜSSEN ZU FUSS ERKLOMMEN WERDEN, UM DEN RUNDETÅRN ZU BESTEIGEN – DER AUSBLICK ÜBER DIE STADT BELOHNT ALLE MÜHE!

Lobby.
The Arne Jacobsen Deluxe Room.
The Nana Ditzel Deluxe room.
Lobby.
Das Arne Jacobsen Deluxe Zimmer.
Das Nanna Ditzel Deluxe Zimmer.

The Finn Juhl Deluxe room.
The 1960's room.
The Jens Risom Deluxe room.
Das Finn Juhl Deluxe Zimmer.
Das 1960er-Jahre-Zimmer.
Das Jens Risom Deluxe-Zimmer.

INFORMATION. ARCHITECTS>
RIEKE GÜNTSCHE ARCHITEKTEN BDA
// CONSTRUCTION 1828, RENOVATION
ALTE GÄRTNEREI 2014 AND KLEINE
SCHÄFEREI 2016. 2 HOUSES> 111 SQM
AND 35 SQM // 4–6 GUESTS AND
2 GUESTS // 3 AND 1 BEDROOMS //
1 BATHROOM EACH.
ADDRESS> IM MOOR 14, BORN,
GERMANY.
WWW.ALTE-GAERTNEREI-BORN.DE

Living room Alte Gärtnerei.
Kleine Schäferei from the garden.
Wohnzimmer Alte Gärtnerei.
Ansicht Kleine Schäferei vom Garten.

Alte Gärtnerei and Kleine Schäferei

BORN, GERMANY |
DEUTSCHLAND

Dating back to 1828, the Alte Gärtnerei with its typical Darss floor plan was carefully restored. The historic building is furnished in a modern style. The living and dining area with a wood stove has large French doors to the terrace and garden. A total of three bedrooms offer space for 2–6 people. The apartment comes with a small sauna. The Kleine Schäferei from about 1900 is a converted and renovated stable with visible brickwork typical of the area and was enlarged with an annex for a sleeping area and bathroom. Lots of light floods the rooms through the glazed doors, and the original wooden doors now serve as folding shutters. The cozy atmosphere comes from a wood stove; the terrace welcomes to sit in the garden among roses and lavender.

Die Alte Gärtnerei aus dem Jahr 1828 mit typischem Darßer Grundriss wurde liebevoll saniert. Die historische Architektur ist modern möbliert. Der Wohn- und Essbereich mit Holzofen öffnet sich mit großen Fenstertüren zur Terrasse und zum Garten. Insgesamt drei Schlafzimmer bieten Platz für 2–6 Personen. Eine kleine Sauna vervollständigt die Wohnung. Die Kleine Schäferei ist ein umgebautes und renoviertes Stallgebäude von ca. 1900 mit ortstypischem Sichtmauerwerk und wurde mit einem Anbau für Schlafraum und Bad erweitert. Verglaste Türöffnungen lassen viel Licht in die Räume, die alten Holztüren dienen nun als Klappläden. Ein Holzofen sorgt für eine gemütliche Atmosphäre, und auf der Terrasse sitzt man im Garten zwischen Rosen und Lavendel.

Exterior view Alte Gärtnerei.
Interior view kitchen.
Außenansicht Alte Gärtnerei.
Innenansicht Küche.

GETTING AROUND. AN EXCELLENT WAY TO EXPLORE THE SURROUNDING MEADOW LANDSCAPES, THE DARSS PRIMEVAL FOREST AND THE SHORELINE ROADS AROUND THE BODDEN LAGOON IS BY BIKE. THE NEIGHBORING BALTIC RESORTS OF WUSTROW, PREROW AND ZINGST OR THE SMALL VILLAGE OF WIECK ARE ALSO ATTRACTIVE DESTINATIONS. WATER SPORTS ENTHUSIASTS WILL FIND GREAT CONDITIONS ON THE BODDEN.

IN DER UMGEBUNG. DIE UMLIEGENDEN WIESENLANDSCHAFTEN, DER DARSSER URWALD UND DIE UFERSTRASSEN UM DEN BODDEN KÖNNEN IDEAL MIT DEM FAHRRAD ERKUNDET WERDEN. AUCH DIE BENACHBARTEN OSTSEEBÄDER WUSTROW, PREROW UND ZINGST ODER DER KLEINE ORT WIECK SIND LOHNENDE ZIELE. UND AUF DEM BODDEN FINDEN WASSERSPORTLER BESTE BEDINGUNGEN.

Living room Kleine Schäferei. Floor plans.
Interior view bedroom.
Wohnzimmer Kleine Schäferei. Grundrisse.
Innenansicht Schlafzimmer.

Living room Alte Gärtnerei. Dining room Kleine
Schäferei. Exterior view from the garden.
Wohnzimmer Alte Gärtnerei. Essbereich Kleine
Schäferei. Außenansicht vom Garten.

INFORMATION. ARCHITECTS>
LIND + ALMOND // 2017.
HOTEL> 2,900 SQM // 100 GUESTS //
54 BEDROOMS // 54 BATHROOMS.
ADDRESS> TORDENSKJOLDSGADE 15,
COPENHAGEN, DENMARK.
WWW.HOTELSANDERS.COM

*A private bedroom. Common dining area.
Interior view.
Privates Schlafzimmer. Gemeinsam Essbereich.
Innenansicht.*

Interior view of the hotel.
The shared living area.
Innenansicht des Hotels.
Gemeinsamer Wohnbereich.

Hotel Sanders

COPENHAGEN, DENMARK |
DÄNEMARK

Parisian flair, British eccentricity, and Far Eastern texture in a Nordic city – Hotel Sanders has all this together under one roof! Its rooms are quiet and offer a retreat from the city's intense life. Restrained colors, high-quality funishings, lovely details such as art and fresh flowers – each room is individually designed, all have in common their sumptuous furnishings and a welcoming and cozy atmosphere. The in-house restaurant, a cocktail bar and rooftop bar satisfy all culinary desires!

Pariser Flair, britische Exzentrik und fernöstliche Textur in einer nordischen Stadt – dies alles vereint das Hotel Sanders unter seinem Dach! Die Gästezimmer sind ruhig, und bieten Rückzug vom Trubel der Stadt. Zurückhaltende Farben, hochwertige Möblierung, liebevolle Details wie Kunst und frische Blumen – jedes Zimmer ist ganz individuell gestaltet, allen gemeinsam ist die luxeriöse Ausstattung und die einladende und gemütliche Atmospäre. Das hauseigene Restaurant, eine Cocktail- und eine Rooftop-Bar lassen auch kulinarisch keine Wünsche offen!

Interior view. Private bedroom. Living area.
Bathroom interior view.
Innenansicht. Privates Schlafzimmer. Wohnbereich.
Innenansicht Badezimmer.

GETTING AROUND. LOCATED IN THE HEART OF COPENHAGEN, SANDERS IS A PERFECT STARTING POINT TO EXPLORE THE BIG CITY. THE PICTURESQUE NYHAVN IS IN CLOSE PROXIMITY. PERSONALIZED BOAT TOURS OF THE HARBOR ON A CLASSIC 1964 MAHOGANY YACHT CAN BE BOOKED AT THE HOTEL.

IN DER UMGEBUNG. IM HERZEN KOPENHAGENS GELEGEN, IST SANDERS PERFEKT POSITIONIERT, UM DIE GROSSE STADT ZU ERKUNDEN. DAS MALERISCHE NYHAVN LIEGT IN DIREKTER NACHBARSCHAFT. EINE INDIVIDUELLE BOOTSTOUR DURCH DEN HAFEN MIT EINER KLASSISCHEN MAHAGONI-YACHT VON 1964 IST IM HOTEL BUCHBAR.

INFORMATION. ARCHITECT>
MARTIN FOCKS // 1999.
7 HOLIDAY APARTMENTS>
FROM 20 TO 100 SQM EACH
APARTMENT // 28 GUESTS //
FROM 1 TO 2 BEDROOMS EACH //
1 BATHROOM EACH.
ADDRESS> DORFSTRASSE 30,
LODDIN, GERMANY.
WWW.ALTE-SCHEUNE-LODDIN.DE

Kitchen and dining area. Sunset.
Exterior view from the garden.
Küchen- und Essbereich. Sonnenuntergang.
Außenansicht vom Garten.

Alte Scheune

LODDIN, GERMANY |
DEUTSCHLAND

The listed building was extended using ecological building materials. Many details link the original character of the listed building with today's demands for high standards of living. Thus, there are thatched roofs and historic beams as well as generous window surfaces that bring a lot of light into the apartments. The Alte Scheune Loddin has been converted into seven vacation rentals ranging from 20 to 100 square meters. Each apartment has its own terrace. In addition, there is a beautiful 2,000-square-meter meadow right next to the reed belt that invites to linger. The direct access to the Achterwasser (backwater) promises a lot of fun swimming.

Das denkmalgeschützte Gebäude wurde unter Verwendung ökologischer Baumaterialien ausgebaut. Zahlreiche Details vermitteln zwischen dem Baudenkmal in seiner Ursprünglichkeit und dem heutigen Anspruch an qualitätvolles Wohnen. So findet sich hier Reetdach und historisches Gebälk genauso wie großzügige Fensterflächen, die viel Licht in die Wohnungen lassen. Aus der Alten Scheune Loddin entstanden so sieben Ferienwohnungen zwischen 20 und 100 qm. Jede Wohnung hat eine eigene Terrasse. Außerdem lädt eine schöne, 2.000 qm große Wiese direkt am Schilfgürtel zum Verweilen ein. Der direkte Zugang zum Achterwasser verspricht großes Badevergnügen.

GETTING AROUND. LODDIN IS SITUATED ON A PROMONTORY BORDERING THE BACKWATER, WITH THE OPEN BALTIC SEA ON THE OTHER SIDE, OFFERING THE BEST CONDITIONS FOR A RELAXING TIME ON AND AROUND WATER. THE CLIFFS ABOVE THE WESTERN SHORE OFFER A MAGNIFICENT PANORAMIC VIEW OF THE PENINSULAS GNITZ AND LIEPER WINKEL AS WELL AS THE MAINLAND COAST OF WESTERN POMERANIA.

IN DER UMGEBUNG. AUF EINER LANDZUNGE DIREKT AN DAS ACHT-ERWASSER GRENZEND, AUF DER ANDEREN SEITE DIE OFFENE OSTSEE, BIETET LODDIN BESTE VORAUSSET-ZUNGEN FÜR ENTSPANNUNG AM UND AUF DEM WASSER. EINEN GROSSARTI-GEN PANORAMABLICK AUF DIE HALB-INSELN GNITZ UND LIEPER WINKEL SOWIE ÜBER DIE VORPOMMERSCHE FESTLANDKÜSTE BIETET DIE STEIL-KÜSTE ÜBER DEM WESTUFER.

View towards the bedroom. Surroundings.
Exterior view. Living area with view to the Baltic Sea.
Blick Richtung Schlafzimmer. Umgebung.
Außenansicht. Wohnbereich mit Blick auf die Ostsee.

Kitchen detail. Exterior view from the garden.
Detail Küche. Außenansicht vom Garten.

INFORMATION. ARCHITECTS>
MAIKE AND RALF HAUG // 2018.
APARTMENT> 130 SQM //
4 GUESTS // 2 BEDROOMS //
ONE AND A HALF BATHROOMS.
ADDRESS> NADELITZ 1, PUTBUS,
RÜGEN, GERMANY.
WWW.LANDLOFT-ILSE.DE

A bedroom. Exterior view.
Interior view of a bathroom. Living room.
Schlafzimmer. Blick von Außen.
Innenansicht Badezimmer. Wohnzimmer.

ilse.dein Landloft

RÜGEN, GERMANY |
DEUTSCHLAND

Landloft ilse was created in the former barns of a 200-year-old farm on the island of Rügen. During its conversion into apartment, emphasis was placed on integrating the existing building as much as possible. Apart from using a wide range of upcycled construction materials, wood and glass were the main materials employed. The result is a loft-style rental for up to 4 people with a small terrace and a garden. Within the apartment itself, only the bedrooms and bathrooms are designed as separate rooms, all other areas are open common spaces. In spring 2022 ilse was extended by a small sauna house and since then, it is a wonderful reason to breathe the Baltic Sea air even during colder periods of the year.

Das Landloft ilse ist in den ehemaligen Stallungen eines 200 Jahre alten Bauernhofes auf der Insel Rügen entstanden. Bei dem Umbau zur Ferienwohnung wurde auf die größtmögliche Einbindung des Bestandes geachtet. Neben zahlreichen upgecycelten Baumaterialien kamen vorrangig Holz und Glas zum Einsatz. Entstanden ist eine Ferienwohnung mit Loft-Charakter für bis zu vier Personen, mit kleiner Terrasse und Garten. In der Wohnung selbst wurden lediglich die Schlafzimmer und Bäder als eigene Räume begrenzt, alle übrigen Bereiche sind als offene Gemeinschaftsflächen gestaltet. Im Frühjahr 2022 wurde ilse um ein kleines Saunahäuschen erweitert und bietet seither eine wunderbare Motivation, sich auch in den kälteren Phasen des Jahres die Ostseeluft um die Nase wehen zu lassen.

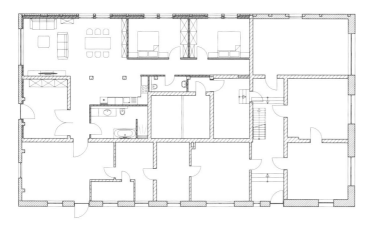

GETTING AROUND. ILSE IS LOCATED IN THE BIOSPHERE RESERVE SOUTH EAST RÜGEN. A BATHING AREA, AN AQUATIC HOLIDAY WORLD WITH A BOAT RENTAL AND THE RASENDER ROLAND LIGHT RAILWAY ARE ONLY A FEW MINUTES AWAY. THE SANDY BEACHES OF THE SEASIDE RESORTS BINZ AND SELLIN ARE ONLY 10 KILOMETERS AWAY. ILSE IS THE IDEAL STARTING POINT FOR CYCLING AND HIKING TOURS OR PADDLING ON THE HOTEL'S OWN STAND-UP BOARDS.

IN DER UMGEBUNG. ILSE LIEGT IM BIOSPHÄREN RESERVAT SÜD OST RÜGEN. EINE BADESTELLE, WASSER-FERIENWELT MIT BOOTSVERLEIH UND DIE KLEINBAHN RASENDER ROLAND SIND IN WENIGEN MINUTEN ERREICH-BAR. DIE SANDSTRÄNDE DER SEEBÄ-DER BINZ UND SELLIN SIND NUR 10 KM ENTFERNT. ILSE IST DAS IDEALE BASISLAGER FÜR RADTOUREN, WAN-DERUNGEN ODER EINEN PADDELTRIP AUF DEN HAUSEIGENEN STAND UP BOARDS.

Kitchen and dining room.
Floor plan. Detail.
Küchen- und Esszimmer.
Grundriss. Detail.

View of the kitchen.
Sauna. Interior view.
Ansicht Küche.
Sauna. Innenansicht.

INFORMATION. DESIGN> FAMILIE BARON VON HOBE-GELTING // CHARLOTTENHUUS 2008, FISCHERKATE 2000, STRANDHOLM 2016. HOUSE AND APARTMENTS> APARTMENT CHARLOTTENHUUS 70 SQM, HOUSE FISCHERKATE 150 SQM AND 3 APARTMENTS STRANDHOLM 60 SQM EACH // 4 GUESTS, 10 GUESTS AND 2 GUESTS EACH // 2 BEDROOMS, 5 BEDROOMS AND 1 BEDROOM EACH // 1 BATHROOM, 2 BATHROOMS AND 1 BATHROOM EACH. ADDRESS> BEVEROE 2–4 AND FALSHÖFT 28, NIEBY, GERMANY. WWW.SCHLOSS-GELTING.DE

Living room Fischerkate cottage. Top view dining area.
Bedroom Fischerkate. Panoramic view.
Wohnzimmer Fischerkate. Essbereich von oben.
Schlafzimmer Fischerkate. Panoramablick.

Ferienhäuser Schloss Gelting

NIEBY, GERMANY | DEUTSCHLAND

The historic vacation homes of Gelting Castle are located next to the nature reserve Geltinger Birk. The charm of past times is combined with modern comfort in a country house style. During the renovation of the houses, the historical character was preserved as much as possible. Thus, there are still original elements of the barn from the 19th century in the thatched fisherman's house. Each of the houses has its own individual character: Strandholm has a romantic garden, the Fischerkate lies in a beautiful solitary location amidst nature, and Charlottenhuus is surrounded by water. Each in and of itself is the perfect place to retreat and enjoy a unique time out.

Direkt an das Naturschutzgebiet Geltinger Birk angrenzend, liegen die historischen Ferienhäuser von Schloss Gelting. Sie vereinen den Charme vergangener Tage mit modernem Komfort im Landhausstil. Bei den Ferienhausrenovierungen wurde der historische Charakter der Häuser weitestgehend erhalten. So finden sich in der reetgedeckten Fischerkate noch Originalelemente des Stalls aus dem 19. Jahrhundert. Jedes der Häuser hat seinen individuellen Charakter: Strandholm mit seinem romantischen Garten, die Fischerkate in traumhafter Alleinlage mitten in der Natur und das Charlottenhuus von Wasser umgeben. Jedes für sich ein perfekter Rückzugsort für eine einzigartige Auszeit.

GETTING AROUND. THE GELTINGER BIRK IS CHARACTERIZED BY MARSHES, SALT MARSHES, SEAGRASS MEADOWS AND DUNES. THE NATURE RESERVE IS HOME TO WILD HORSES, GALLOWAYS AND UP TO 200 SPECIES OF BIRDS. NATURE LOVERS GET THEIR MONEY'S WORTH NEXT DOOR. BEACHES AND THE BALTIC SEA ATTRACT FAMILIES, WATER ENTHUSIASTS AND KITE SURFERS.

IN DER UMGEBUNG. SÜMPFE, SALZ-, SEEGRASWIESEN UND DÜNEN PRÄGEN DIE GELTINGER BIRK. WILD-PFERDE UND GALLOWAYS GRASEN IM NATURSCHUTZGEBIET, DAS BIS ZU 200 VOGELARTEN LEBENSRAUM BIETET. NATURLIEBHABER KOMMEN DIREKT VOR DER TÜR AUF IHRE KOSTEN. STRÄNDE UND OSTSEE LOCKEN AUSSERDEM FAMILIEN, WASSERSPORT-LER UND KITESURFER.

Fischerkate from the garden. Living room
Charlottenhuus. Bedroom Strandholm.
Fischerkate vom Garten. Wohnzimmer
Charlottenhuus. Schlafzimmer Strandholm.

Interior view Strandholm.
Charlottenhuus' terrace with view of the
Baltic Sea. Exterior view Strandholm.
Innenansicht Strandholm.
Terrasse Charlottenhuus mit
Ostseeblick. Außenansicht Strandholm.

INFORMATION. ARCHITECTS> SIEGEL ARCHITECTURE // 2017. APARTEMENTS AND HOTEL ROOMS> 3,922 SQM // 2–4 GUESTS EACH // 1–2 BEDROOMS // 1 BATHROOM. ADDRESS> LILLA VARVSGATAN 24, MALMÖ, SWEDEN. WWW.OHBOY.SE

Hotel entrance from South. Sleeping area in concrete and ash wood. Hotel room with kitchen area upstairs and sleeping area downstairs.
Hoteleingang von Süden. Der Schlafbereich mit Beton und Eschenholz. Hotelzimmer mit Küchenbereich im Obergeschoss und Schlafbereich im Erdgeschoss.

OHBOY!
The Bicycle
House

MALMÖ, SWEDEN | SCHWEDEN

Coziness on the first floor and the best view from the second level – the loft-like rooms over two floors unite these two qualities of living. These two floors make it possible to accommodate many functions in a small space. On the first floor there are a bathroom, closet and three sleeping places. The kitchen, dining area, and a working space with a view of the greenery are located on the second floor. The rooms are characterized by wood, concrete, and a restrained color palette. The furnishings are all locally anchored, designed, produced, and made from southern Sweden materials. The furniture was created and manufactured in the region, and the ash and oak wood used comes from the immediate surroundings. Centrally located in Malmö, this little courtyard full of bamboo offers privacy and a break from the hustle and bustle of the city.

Gemütlichkeit im Erdgeschoss und beste Aussicht von der zweiten Ebene – die loftartigen Zimmer über zwei Etagen verbinden beide Wohnqualitäten. Die zwei Geschosse ermöglichen es, viele Funktionen auf kleinem Raum unterzubringen. Im Erdgeschoss finden sich Bad, Kleiderschrank und drei Schlafplätze. Im Obergeschoss befindet sich die Küche, der Essbereich sowie ein Arbeitsbereich mit Blick ins Grüne. Holz, Beton und eine zurückhaltende Farbpalette prägen die Zimmer. Die Ausstattung ist lokal verankert: Design, Produktion und Materialien aus Süd-Schweden. Die Möbel wurden in der Region entworfen und gefertigt, das verbaute Eschen- und Eichenholz stammt aus direkter Umgebung. Zentral gelegen in Malmö, bietet der kleine Innenhof mit üppigem Bambusbestand Privatsphäre und Abstand zum urbanen Trubel.

*Front view with one of the biggest
skateparks in Europe, the "Stapelbäddsparken".
Floor plans of the hotel rooms.
Frontansicht mit einem der größten
Skateparks Europas „Stapelbäddsparken".
Grundrisse der Hotelzimmer.*

First floor with extra bed under the staircase.
Hotel room with view
of the bamboo garden in the backyard.
Erdgeschoss mit Zusatzbett unter der Treppe.
Hotelzimmer mit Blick
auf den Bambusgarten im Hinterhof.

GETTING AROUND. WHEN YOU STEP OUT OF THE DOOR, YOU FIND YOURSELF IN THE CENTER OF MALMÖ. FROM THERE, YOU CAN EXPLORE THE CITY EITHER ON FOOT OR BY BIKE – WHICH IS INCLUDED IN THE HOTEL RENT – FOR EXAMPLE THE PRETTY OLD TOWN "GAMLA STADEN". A VISIT TO THE MODERNA MUSEET IS ALSO WORTHWHILE. THE SEA AND THE BEACH ARE ALSO JUST AROUND THE CORNER!

IN DER UMGEBUNG. TRITT MAN VOR DIE TÜR, BEFINDET MAN SICH BEREITS IM ZENTRUM VON MALMÖ. VON HIER AUS LÄSST SICH DIE STADT ZU FUSS ODER PER FAHRRAD ERKUNDEN – WAS IN DER HOTELMIETE ENTHALTEN IST, ZUM BEISPIEL DIE HÜBSCHE ALTSTADT „GAMLA STADEN". LOHNEND IST EBENFALLS EIN BESUCH DES MODERNA MUSEET. AUCH DAS MEER UND DER STRAND SIND GLEICH UM DIE ECKE!

INFORMATION. ARCHITECTS> WACKER ZEIGER ARCHITEKTEN // 2008. HOLIDAY HOME> 75 SQM // CA. 6 GUESTS // 2 BEDROOMS + 1 IN AN OUTBUILDING // 2 BATHROOMS. ADDRESS> STRASSE ZUM MEER 10, LUBMIN, GERMANY. WWW.OSTSEE-URLAUB-LUBMIN.DE

Side view. External perspective.
Façade detail.
Seitenansicht. Außenperspektive.
Detail Fassade.

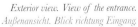

Exterior view. View of the entrance.
Außenansicht. Blick richtung Eingang

Meerhaus Lubmin

LUBMIN, GERMANY |
DEUTSCHLAND

This small wooden holiday home stands under pine trees within sight of the Baltic Sea. Contrary to the architecture imitating Heiligendamm next door, it maintains a more modest but at the same time self-confident "dacha culture". The interior is at once spacious and compact. The attic faces the living and dining room on the first floor like a gallery. If more than 6 people need accommodation there are extra sleeping places in an outbuilding on site. The house is heated by an air-heating pump. On cold summer days the soapstone stove is on.

In Sichtkontakt zur Ostsee steht unter Kiefern dieses kleine Holz-Ferienhaus. Antithetisch zu den Heiligendamm-Nacheiferern nebenan behauptet es eine bescheidenere, zugleich selbstbewusste „Datscha-Kultur". Großzügig und kompakt zugleich präsentiert sich der Innenraum. Das Dachgeschoss steht galerieartig zum Wohn- und Esszimmer im Erdgeschoss. Wenn mehr als sechs Personen unterkommen sollen, gibt es noch Schlafplätze in einem Nebengelass auf dem Grundstück. Das Haus wird mit einer Luft-Wärmepumpe beheizt. An kalten Sommertagen wird der Speckofen angemacht.

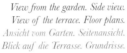

View from the garden. Side view.
View of the terrace. Floor plans.
Ansicht vom Garten. Seitenansicht.
Blick auf die Terrasse. Grundrisse.

GETTING AROUND. IT TAKES ONLY 1 MINUTE FROM THE FRONT DOOR TO THE WATER OF THE BALTIC SEA. DEPENDING ON THE WEATHER, YOU CAN SEE OR GLIMPSE THE ISLAND OF RÜGEN (ABOUT 20 KILOMETERS AWAY). THE GREIFSWALDER BODDEN IS A GREAT PLACE FOR SWIMMING, SURFING AND SAILING. OTHERWISE, YOU CAN TAKE WALKS ON THE BEACH OR IN THE ADJOINING PINE FOREST.

IN DER UMGEBUNG. VON DER HAUSTÜR BIS INS WASSER DER OSTSEE BRAUCHT MAN 1 MINUTE. JE NACH WETTER SIEHT BZW. ERAHNT MAN VON DORT AUS DIE INSEL RÜGEN (CA. 20 KM ENTFERNT). DER GREIFSWALDER BODDEN LÄDT ZUM SCHWIMMEN, SURFEN UND SEGELN EIN. SONST UN-TERNIMMT MAN SPAZIERGÄNGE AM STRAND ODER IM ANGRENZENDEN KIEFERNWALD.

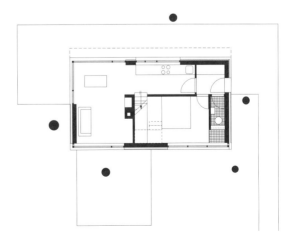

INFORMATION. ARCHITECTS>
AGMM ARCHITEKTEN, MATTHIAS
ARNDT // 2020. HOUSE> 164 SQM //
8 GUESTS // 4 BEDROOMS //
2 BATHROOMS.
ADDRESS> MEERLEBEN 1,
HOHENKIRCHEN, GERMANY.
WWW.MEERLEBEN-FERIENDORF.DE/
FERIENHAUS/NURSO/

Interior view of the living room. South-West view.
House Nurso at night.
Innenansicht Wohnzimmer. Außenansicht Süd-West.
Haus Nurso mit Abendstimmung.

Haus Nurso

HOHENKIRCHEN OT NIENDORF,
GERMANY | DEUTSCHLAND

Haus Nurso offers a lot of space for large families or groups of friends: the big dining table, four bedrooms with box-spring beds and 150 square meters of well-defined and minimalist designed living space are the perfect invitation to have big get-togethers. The large living, cooking and dining area with gallery and fireplace, or one of the three outdoor terraces, are the perfect place for socializing, while the sauna and bathtub with views to the garden and over the fields may serve as retreats. The entire interior is designed in Scandinavian style with a subtle color palette and with great attention to detail. The lighting in the house is mainly indirect via light coves.

Haus Nurso bietet reichlich Platz für große Familien oder Freundesgruppen: Der großen Esstisch, vier Schlafzimmer mit Boxspringbetten und 150 qm klar und minimalistisch gestaltete Wohnfläche laden ein zu großen Runden. Geselliges Zusammensein im großzügigen Wohn-, Koch- und Essbereich mit Galerie und Kamin oder auf einer der drei Außenterrassen ist genauso möglich wie Rückzug in die Sauna oder die Badewanne mit Blick in den Garten und übers Feld. Skandinavisches Design in zurückhaltender Farbpalette zieht sich mit viel Liebe zum Detail durch die gesamte Einrichtung. Die Beleuchtung im Haus erfolgt überwiegend indirekt durch Lichtvouten.

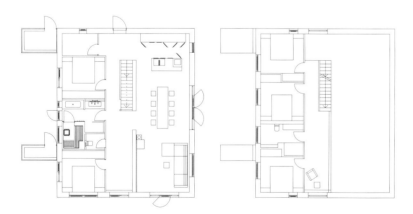

GETTING AROUND. THE BALTIC SEA BEACH IS JUST A 10-MINUTE WALK AWAY. THE LONG BAY WOHLENBERGER WIEK INVITES TO TAKE A WALK, HAVE A PICNIC ON THE BEACH OR DO SPORTS. IT IS STILL RATHER UNSPOILED. THE BAY IS GOOD PLACE FOR CHILDREN AS THE WATER IS VERY SHALLOW. THE OLD TOWN OF WISMAR IS ONLY 15 KILOMETERS AND SCHWERIN CASTLE IS 45 KILOMETERS AWAY.

IN DER UMGEBUNG. ZUM STRAND AN DER OSTSEEKÜSTE SIND ES GERADE EINMAL 10 GEHMINUTEN. DIE LANG-GEZOGENE BUCHT WOHLENBERGER WIEK LÄDT ZU SPAZIERGÄNGEN, EINEM PICKNICK AM STRAND ODER SPORTLICHEN AKTIVITÄTEN EIN. SIE IST NOCH RELATIV NATURBELAS-SEN. FÜR DEN STRANDBESUCH MIT KINDERN HERVORRAGEND GEEIGNET, DA DAS WASSER SEHR SEICHT IST. ZUR WISMARER ALTSTADT SIND ES NUR 15 KM UND BIS ZUM SCHWERINER SCHLOSS 45 KM.

South-East view from the garden.
Floor plans. Bedroom.
Außenansicht Süd-Ost vom Garten.
Grundrisse. Schlafzimmer.

Hallway window with seat. Dining area.
Exterior view from the garden.
Flur mit Sitzfenster. Essbereich.
Außenansicht vom Garten.

INFORMATION. ARCHITECT>
SUSANNE KAISER // 2018.
BOUTIQUEHOTEL> 1,978 SQM //
65 GUESTS // 29 BEDROOMS //
29 BATHROOMS.
ADDRESS> KULMSTRASSE 6, SEEBAD
HERINGSDORF, USEDOM, GERMANY.
WWW.BOJE06.DE

A bedroom. Details.
Interior view of the dining area.
Schlafzimmer. Details.
Innenansicht Essbereich.

Boje06

USEDOM, GERMANY |
DEUTSCHLAND

Where once there was a school desk and blackboard, nowadays it's just okay to play hooky. 29 cabins and berths provide a perfect place for singles, couples, and small families to lay down during their break on Usedom. Generous picture motifs, furniture made of wood and steel in vintage style as well as comfortable armchairs make it truly favorite places. Timeless design with maritime charm, individual vacation dreams that become reality. In addition, the host family Wehrmann is offering a courteous and at the same time unobtrusive service. There are many places to enjoy and experience in this small, family-run "resort" – its in-house spa and gym, a restaurant for breakfast, a food container, two restaurants and a beach lounge right in front of or next door to the hotel.

Wo einst Schulbank und Tafel standen, darf man heute einfach mal blau machen. 29 Kabinen und Kojen bieten Singles, Paaren und kleinen Familien einen perfekten Liegeplatz während des Urlaubs auf Usedom. Großzügige Bildmotive, Möbel aus Holz und Stahl im Retrolook sowie bequeme Sessel machen sie zu echten Lieblingsorten. Zeitloses Design in maritimem Charme, individuelle Ferienträume, die Wirklichkeit werden. Dazu kombiniert die Gastgeberfamilie Wehrmann einen zuvorkommenden und zugleich unaufdringlichen Service. Hauseigenes Spa & Gym, Frühstücksrestaurant, Foodcontainer sowie zwei Restaurants und die Strandlounge direkt gegenüber bzw. nebenan – Genuss- und Erlebnisorte gibt es in dem kleinen familiären „Resort" viele.

GETTING AROUND. INDIVIDUAL LIVING NEAR THE BEACH AND PIER. THE SEASIDE RESORT IS LOCATED ON ONE OF THE MOST BEAUTIFUL STRETCHES OF BEACH ON THE ISLAND. SPECIAL FEATURES ARE THE VILLAS IN THE STYLE OF SPA ARCHITECTURE AND THE LONGEST BEACH PROMENADE OF EUROPE. BESIDES THE BEACH, THE FASCINATING LANDSCAPE OF THE HINTERLAND INCLUDING THE BACKWATER AND THE COASTAL FORESTS INVITE TO DISCOVERY.

IN DER UMGEBUNG. INDIVIDUELLES WOHNEN IN UNMITTELBARER NÄHE ZU STRAND UND SEEBRÜCKE. DAS SEEBAD LIEGT AN EINEM DER SCHÖNSTEN STRANDABSCHNITTE DER INSEL. BESONDERE MERKMALE SIND DIE VILLEN IM STIL DER BÄDERARCHITEKTUR UND DIE LÄNGSTE STRANDPROMENADE EUROPAS. NEBEN DEM STRAND LADEN AUCH DAS LANDSCHAFTLICH FASZINIERENDE HINTERLAND SAMT ACHTERWASSER UND DIE KÜSTENWÄLDER ZU ENTDECKUNGEN EIN.

Exterior view. Floor plan showroom.
Interior view hallway.
Außenansicht. Grundriss Musterzimmer.
Innenansicht Flur.

Detail. Gym area. Sauna.
Detail. Gymbereich. Sauna.

INFORMATION. ARCHITECTS>
MEYER TERHORST ARCHITEKTEN //
2020. APARTMENTS> 260 SQM //
10 GUESTS // 5 BEDROOMS //
4 BATHROOMS.
ADDRESS> MÜHLENSTRASSE 16,
WAABS, GERMANY.
WWW.ELSASENKEL.DE

Kitchen of apartments Meta and Ida.
Interior view of the sauna. Street view of apartments
Lotte and Gesa.
Küche Wohnung Meta und Ida.
Innenansicht Sauna. Straßenansicht Wohnung
Lotte und Gesa.

Open-plan kitchen Lotte.
Exterior view of the sauna.
Wohnküche Wohnung Lotte.
Außenansicht Sauna.

Elsas Enkel

WAABS, GERMANY |
DEUTSCHLAND

Elsas Enkel is located in Klein Waabs – close to the Baltic Sea, right between Eckernförde and Kappeln. There are four individual apartments in the birthplace of grandmother Elsa, plus a new forge. They are embedded in a beautiful garden that blooms at any time of the year. The apartments have one thing in common – high quality. The interior was made focusing on natural materials and modern furnishings. The kitchens are equipped to a high standard; the apartments come with cozy fireplaces and small private terrace. A brine-water heat pump in combination with a photovoltaic system and battery storage were chosen, making this vacation complex an energy-efficient and sustainably oriented project. The freestanding sauna in the garden completes this object.

In Klein Waabs an der Ostsee – zwischen Eckernförde und Kappeln – befindet sich Elsas Enkel. Hier wurden vier individuelle Ferienwohnungen im Geburtshaus der Großmutter Elsa sowie eine neue Schmiede gebaut und eingebettet in einen wunderschönen Garten, der zu jeder Jahreszeit blüht. Allen Wohnungen gemein ist die hohe Qualität. Bei der Einrichtung wurde Wert gelegt auf natürliche Materialien und moderne Möblierung. Die Küchen sind hochwertig ausgestattet, die Wohnungen haben gemütliche Öfen und eine eigene kleine Terrasse. Eine Sole-Wasser-Wärmepumpe in Kombination mit einer Photovoltaikanlage und Batteriespeicher wurden gewählt und machen diese Ferienanlage zu einem energieeffizienten und nachhaltig ausgerichteten Projekt. Die freistehende Sauna im Garten rundet das Objekt ab.

Garden view. Bathroom of apartment Meta.
Floor plan. Main entrance of Elsas Enkel.
Gartenansicht. Bad Wohnung Meta.
Grundriss Erdgeschoss. Haupteingang Elsas Enkel.

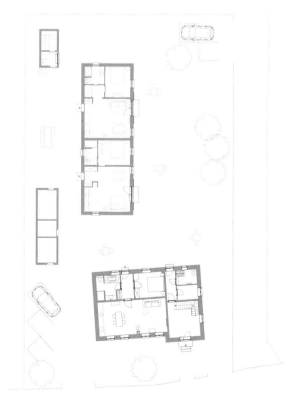

GETTING AROUND. THERE ARE LOTS OF ACTIVITY OPTIONS IN THE SURROUNDING AREA: HIKING ALONG THE BALTIC SEA OR THE SCHLEI TRAILS, AN EXCELLENT NETWORK OF CYCLING PATHS, HORSE RIDING NEARBY, AND WATER SPORTS ON THE BALTIC SEA. A STROLL THROUGH THE WEEKLY MARKET IN ECKERNFÖRDE IS THE PLEASANT ALTERNATIVE!

IN DER UMGEBUNG. DIE UMGEBUNG LÄDT ZU VIEL AKTIVITÄT EIN: WANDER-MÖGLICHKEITEN AM OSTSEESTRAND ODER ÜBER DIE SCHLEIWANDERWEGE, EIN SEHR GUT AUSGEBAUTES FAHR-RADWEGENETZ, REITMÖGLICHKEITEN IN DER NÄHE, UND WASSERSPORT AN DER OSTSEE. DIE GEMÜTLICHE ALTERNATIVE: EIN BUMMEL ÜBER DEN WOCHENMARKT IN ECKERNFÖRDE!

INFORMATION. INTERIOR ARCHITECTS> CO.DESIGNSTUDIO & BARBARA B. BECKER // 2018. HOTEL> 9,000 SQM // 395 GUESTS // 234 BEDROOMS // 234 BATHROOMS. ADDRESS> ODEONS KVARTER 11, ODENSE, DENMARK. WWW.HOTELODEON.DK

Interior view of Hotel Odeon. Common dining area.
Interior view of a hotel room.
Innenansicht Hotel Odeon. Gemeinsamer Essbereich.
Innenansicht Hotelzimmer.

Hotel Odeon

ODENSE, DENMARK | DÄNEMARK

Hotel Odeon is located in the center of the Hans Christian Andersen district in Odense. The hotel's design is influenced by Nordic aesthetics: the love of craftsmanship and the elegance of Danish furniture design. Carefully selected furniture and carpets, natural materials such as stone, and carefully selected patterns and color palettes in soft tones create a warm, elegant atmosphere. All materials used are of high quality, and the furnishings and lighting are complemented with Danish design classics and individual art. In the rooms, as well as in the lobby, in the hotel's own restaurant H.C by Meyers , in the bar or by the fireplace, the emphasis is on comfort.

Im Zentrum des Hans-Christian-Andersen-Viertels in Odense liegt das Hotel Odeon. Das Design des Hotels ist von der nordischen Ästhetik geprägt: der Liebe zur Handwerkskunst und der Eleganz des dänischen Möbeldesigns. Sorgfältig ausgewählte Möbel und Teppiche, natürliche Materialien wie Stein und fein abgestimmte Muster und Farbpaletten in sanften Tönen sorgen für eine warme, elegante Atmosphäre. Alle verwendeten Materialien sind hochwertig, die Möblierung und Beleuchtung mit dänischen Design-Klassikern und individueller Kunst ergänzt. Der Komfort steht in den Zimmern im Vordergrund und setzt sich in der Lobby, im hoteleigenen Restaurant H.C by Meyers , in der Bar oder am Kamin fort.

Relaxation area with fireplace.
Interior view of a suite.
Entspannungsbereich mit Kamin.
Innenansicht Suite.

Hotel room. Detail.
View of the conference room.
Hotelzimmer. Detail.
Blick in den Konferenzraum.

GETTING AROUND. IN ODENSE YOU CAN FOLLOW IN THE FOOTSTEPS OF HANS CHRISTIAN ANDERSEN – HIS BIRTHPLACE, A MUSEUM AND A FAIRY-TALE SCULPTURE PARK PAY TRIBUTE TO THE ARTIST. THE PICTURESQUE OLD TOWN CAN BE EXPLORED ON FOOT. THE EXHIBITIONS OF MODERN ART AT THE BRANDTS ART MUSEUM ARE WORTH SEEING.

IN DER UMGEBUNG. IN ODENSE LÄSST SICH AUF DEN SPUREN VON HANS CHRISTIAN ANDERSEN WAN-DELN – SEIN GEBURTSHAUS, EIN MUSEUM UND EIN MÄRCHENHAFTER SKULPTURENPARK WÜRDIGEN DEN KÜNSTLER. DIE MALERISCHE ALTSTADT KANN ZU FUSS ERKUNDET WERDEN. SEHENSWERT SIND DIE AUSSTEL-LUNGEN ZU MODERNER KUNST IM BRANDTS KUNSTMUSEUM.

INFORMATION. ARCHITECTS>
SUNDER-PLASSMANN ARCHITEKTEN
// 2021. 5 APARTMENTS> CA. 100 SQM
EACH // 4 GUESTS PER APARTMENT //
2 BEDROOMS EACH // 1 BATHROOM.
ADDRESS> HAFEN 19 D, KAPPELN,
GERMANY.
WWW.NETZSCHUPPEN.NET

Kitchen and dining area. Exterior view.
Interior view of the sleeping area.
Küche und Essbereich. Außenansicht.
Innenansicht Schlafbereich.

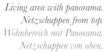

Living area with panorama.
Netzschuppen from top.
Wohnbereich mit Panorama.
Netzschuppen von oben.

Netzschuppen

KAPPELN, GERMANY | DEUTSCHLAND

The unique Netzschuppen loft houses are in Kappeln, next to the beautiful Schlei river overlooking the fishing harbor. Inspired by this location, the five award-winning houses were designed in the style of Scandinavian fishnet sheds. The interior welcomes architecture lovers and people who want to observe and enjoy the hustle and bustle of the harbor with its cozy loft character. The light-flooded rooms feature high-end interiors designed in light colors and warm, natural materials, as well as individually selected furniture. There are four mezzanine floors on more than 100 square meters, a large living-dining room with kitchen, two bedrooms, a shower room, and an extra toilet. You can park your car directly on the open first floor.

Die unvergleichlichen Netzschuppen-Lofthäuser liegen in Kappeln, direkt an der schönen Schlei mit Blick auf den Fischereihafen. Von dieser Lage inspiriert, wurden die fünf preisgekrönten Häuser im Stil skandinavischer Netzschuppen entworfen. Das Innere wartet mit hyggeligem Loftcharakter auf Architektur-Liebhaber und Menschen, die das Treiben am Hafen beobachten und genießen wollen. Die lichtdurchfluteten Räume mit ihrer hochwertigen Innenausstattung wurden in hellen Farben und warmen, natürlichen Materialien sowie individuell ausgewählten Möbeln gestaltet. Auf vier Halbgeschossen befinden sich auf über 100 qm ein großer Wohn-Essraum mit Küche, zwei Schlafzimmer, Duschbad und ein extra WC. Ihr Fahrzeug parken Sie direkt im offenen Erdgeschoss.

Interior view of the living and dining area.
A bedroom.
Innenansicht Wohn- und Essbereich.
Schlafzimmer.

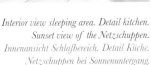

Interior view sleeping area. Detail kitchen.
Sunset view of the Netzschuppen.
Innenansicht Schlafbereich. Detail Küche.
Netzschuppen bei Sonnenuntergang.

GETTING AROUND. THE NETZSCHUP-
PEN LOFT HOUSES ARE LOCATED
BY THE HARBOR AND YET CLOSE TO
THE CITY CENTER. THE SCHLEI RIVER
OFFERS THE BEST CONDITIONS FOR
MANY DIFFERENT WATER SPORTS. THE
REGION OF THE SCHLEI IS AN INVITA-
TION TO GO ON DISCOVERY TOURS
AND THE BALTIC SEA COAST CAN
ALSO BE REACHED IN NO TIME. THE
CHARMING KAPPELN CITY CENTER
WITH ITS VARIED SHOPPING OPPORTU-
NITIES IS JUST A FEW STEPS AWAY.

IN DER UMGEBUNG. DIE NETZSCHUP-
PEN-LOFTHÄUSER LIEGEN DIREKT AM
HAFEN UND ZUGLEICH ZENTRUMS-
NAH. DIE SCHLEI BIETET BESTE BEDIN-
GUNGEN FÜR VIELSEITIGEN WASSER-
SPORT. DIE SCHLEIREGION LÄDT ZU
ERKUNDUNGSTOUREN EIN UND AUCH
DIE OSTSEEKÜSTE IST SCHNELL ER-
REICHT. DIE CHARMANTE KAPPELNER
INNENSTADT MIT ABWECHSLUNGSREI-
CHEN EINKAUFSMÖGLICHKEITEN IST
NUR WENIGE SCHRITTE ENTFERNT.

INFORMATION. ARCHITECTS>
MÖHRING ARCHITEKTEN // 2015.
HOUSE> 130 SQM // 4–6 GUESTS //
2 BEDROOMS // 2 BATHROOMS.
ADDRESS> KIELSTRASSE 11,
WIECK, GERMANY.
WWW.WIECKIN.DE

Living and dining area. Sauna.
Exterior view from the garden.
Wohn- und Essbereich. Sauna.
Außenansicht vom Garten.

WIECKin

WIECK, GERMANY |
DEUTSCHLAND

The new house is built in a typical local construction style and color scheme with jamb walls. The design language of a traditional barn is interpreted in a modern way by means of a dark larch wood façade, a folded zinc roof and large windows. The first floor offers a spacious room with a cozy fireplace and lounge area. The interior of the house is functional and simple, modern and of excellent quality. Minimalist design and a consistent color scheme are common to all the house's exclusive furnishings. Contrasting with the dark façade, the white walls and warm wood give the entire interior space a radiant glow. The light-flooded bedrooms provide fantastic views of the green surroundings. The large bathroom with built-in sauna is in line with the rest of the house in terms of design and comfort.

Das Ferienhaus folgt der regional typischen Bauform und Farbgestaltung eines Drempelhauses. Die Formensprache einer traditionellen Scheune wird mit der dunklen Lärchenholzfassade, dem Zinkfalzdach und großen Fenstern modern interpretiert. Das Erdgeschoss bietet einen großzügigen Raum mit gemütlichem Kamin- und Sitzbereich. Die Einrichtung des Hauses ist funktional schlicht, modern und hochwertig. Die reduzierte Form- und Farbgebung zieht sich durch die exklusive Ausstattung des Hauses. Kontrastierend zur dunklen Fassade strahlt der gesamte Innenraum mit seinen weißen Wänden und seinem warmen Holz. Die lichtgefluteten Schlafzimmer gewähren fantastische Ausblicke in die Umgebung. Das große Badezimmer mit integrierter Sauna steht dem Rest des Hauses in Sachen Design und Komfort in nichts nach.

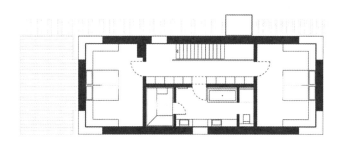

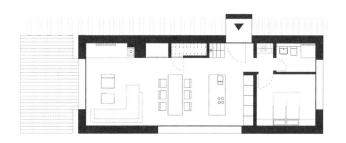

GETTING AROUND. THERE ARE MANY PLACES TO ENJOY: THE NATURE OF THE DARSS NATIONAL PARK, THE BEAUTIFUL WEST BEACH, THE ARTISTS' COLONY OF AHRENSHOOP, THE CHARMING SPA TOWN OF ZINGST. THE SEASIDE RESORTS AND BEACHES ARE EASY TO REACH BY BIKE. THE BODSTEDTER BODDEN LAGOON IS VERY CLOSE, AND THE BALTIC SEA IS GREAT FOR WATER SPORTS: FISHING, KITE SURFING AND SAILING, DIVING OR SURFING.

IN DER UMGEBUNG. DIE NATUR IM NATIONALPARK DARSS, DER TRAUM-HAFTE WESTSTRAND, DIE KÜNST-LERKOLONIE AHRENSHOOP, DAS CHARMANTE HEILBAD ZINGST – VIELE BESONDERE ORTE WARTEN AUF DEN BESUCH. DIE OSTSEEBÄDER UND STRÄNDE SIND MIT DEM FAHRRAD SCHNELL ERREICHT. DER BODSTEDTER BODDEN LIEGT IN DIREKTER NACH-BARSCHAFT, UND DIE OSTSEE BIETET BESTE MÖGLICHKEITEN ZUM WASSER-SPORT: ANGELN, KITEN UND SEGELN, TAUCHEN ODER SURFEN.

Living room with fireplace and garden view.
Floor plans first floor and second floor.
A bedroom.
Wohnzimmer mit Kamin und Gartenblick.
Grundrisse Erdgeschoss und 1.Obergeschoss.
Schlafzimmer.

Side view form the garden.
Interior view.
Seitenansicht vom Garten.
Innenansicht.

INFORMATION. INTERIOR
ARCHITECTS> JOI DESIGN //
1850, SANIERUNG 2017.
BOUTIQUE HOTEL> 1,900 SQM //
60 GUESTS // 30 BEDROOMS //
30 BATHROOMS.
ADDRESS> AM LEUCHTTURM 16,
ROSTOCK-WARNEMÜNDE, GERMANY.
WWW.HOTEL-AM-LEUCHTTURM.DE

Interior view hotel room. Detail. Breakfast lounge.
Exterior view of Hotel am Leuchtturm.
Innenansicht Hotel Zimmer. Detail. Frühstückslounge.
Außenansicht Hotel am Leuchtturm.

Hotel Am Leuchtturm

ROSTOCK-WARNEMÜNDE, GERMANY | DEUTSCHLAND

The privately run hotel is one of the oldest hotels in Warnemünde and was extensively modernized and expanded in 2017. "Feel at home on vacation" is the intention of the design concept throughout the house. 30 comfortable, light-flooded rooms offer dreamlike views. Luxurious bathrooms show up in black and white with the most modern sanitary equipment. The new veranda-style extension houses the reception and lobby with glass fireplace and library, as well as the elegant breakfast lounge with a view of the dunes. Natural materials in interplay with the colors blue and white in front of restrained surfaces of stained oak are the design's main protagonists. Pictures and sculptures of local artists as well as historical photographs underline the family flair of the entire house.

Das privat geführte Hotel ist eines der ältesten Hotels in Warnemünde und wurde 2017 aufwendig modernisiert und erweitert. „Im Urlaub wie zu Hause fühlen" ist die Intention des Designkonzeptes im gesamten Haus. 30 komfortable, lichtdurchflutete Zimmer versprechen traumhafte Ausblicke. Luxuriöse Badezimmer zeigen sich in Schwarz-Weiß mit modernster Sanitärausstattung. Der neue Anbau im Verandastil beherbergt die Rezeption und Lobby mit Glaskamin und Bibliothek, als auch die elegante Frühstückslounge mit Blick auf die Dünen. Natürliche Materialien im Zusammenspiel mit den Farben Blau und Weiß vor zurückhaltenden Flächen aus gebeizter Eiche sind Hauptdarsteller im Design. Bilder und Skulpturen lokaler Künstler sowie historische Aufnahmen unterstreichen das familiäre Flair des gesamten Hauses.

Lobby with fireplace.
Hotel room with sea view.
Lobby mit Kamin.
Hotel Zimmer mit Meerblick.

Interior view of the lobby. Bathroom.
Hallways of Hotel am Leuchtturm.
Innenansicht Lobby. Badezimmer.
Hotel am Leuchtturm Flure.

GETTING AROUND. THE FANTASTIC LOCATION, RIGHT ON THE PROMENADE AND ONLY A FEW STEPS FROM THE BEACH, PUTS THE GUEST STRAIGHT IN THE CENTER OF THE FORMER FISHING VILLAGE. NEARBY IS THE "OLD STREAM" WITH ITS TRADITONAL HOUSES AND FISHING BOATS. SMALL ALLEYS AND THE BREAKWATER, AS WELL AS RESTAURANTS AND CAFES INVITE TO LINGER.

IN DER UMGEBUNG. DIE TRAUMHAFTE LAGE, DIREKT AUF DER PROMENADE UND NUR WENIGE SCHRITTE VOM STRAND ENTFERNT, LÄSST DEN GAST UNMITTELBAR IM ZENTRUM DES EHEMALIGEN FISCHERDORFES SEIN. IN DER NÄHE BEFINDET SICH DER „ALTE STROM" MIT SEINEN HISTORISCHEN HÄUSERN UND DEN TRADITIONELLEN FISCHKUTTERN. KLEINE GASSEN UND DIE MOLE, SOWIE RESTAURANTS UND CAFÉS LADEN ZUM VERWEILEN EIN.

INFORMATION. ARCHITECT> GREGOR HERBERHOLZ // 2014. HOUSE> 40 SQM // 4 GUESTS // 2 BEDROOMS // 1 BATHROOM. ADDRESS> FELDWEG 29, OSTSEEBAD AHRENSHOOP, GERMANY.

Kitchen and living area. Window with bench.
Exterior view of the passageway.
Küchen- und Wohnbereich. Fenster mit Sitzbank.
Durchgang Außenansicht.

microHOME

AHRENSHOOP, GERMANY |
DEUTSCHLAND

microHOME's clearly defined structure is clad in a façade of untreated larch wood slats. Huge wood windows create light-flooded rooms, a floor-to-ceiling glazing to the terrace connects the indoor and outdoor spaces. A large bench on the south side of the living room invites guests to linger at any time of the year, establishing visual contact with the meadow landscapes surrounding the house and making it possible to feel nature indoors as well. To realize a living room as large as possible on only 40 square meters of living space, the size of the two bedrooms was kept to a minimum. Moreover, the bathroom and kitchen facilities got a compact unit in the central part of the house. During the whole construction, the emphasis was placed on the use of natural materials.

Der klar strukturierte Baukörper des microHOME wird von einer Fassade aus unbehandelten Lärchenholzleisten bekleidet. Große Holzfenster lassen lichtdurchflutete Räume entstehen, eine bodentiefe Verglasung zur Terrasse schafft eine Verbindung zwischen Wohn- und Außenraum. Die großzügige Sitzbank auf der Südseite des Wohnraums lädt zu jeder Jahreszeit zum Verweilen ein, schafft Blickbeziehungen zu den umliegenden Wiesenlandschaften und macht die Natur auch im Haus erlebbar. Um auf nur 40 qm Wohnfläche einen möglichst großzügigen Wohnraum zu realisieren, wurde die Größe der beiden Schlafräume auf ein Minimum begrenzt. Zudem wurden Bad und Küche kompakt in der Mitte des Hauses zusammengefasst. Bei dem gesamten Bau wurde großer Wert auf den Einsatz natürlicher Materialen gelegt.

GETTING AROUND. IT'S ONLY A FEW MINUTES WALK FROM MICROHOME TO THE BALTIC SEA BEACH AND THE BODDEN LAGOON. THE ART MUSEUM AHRENSHOOP IS ONLY AT WALK DISTANCE. THE NATIONAL PARK VORPOMMERSCHE BODDEN-LANDSCHAFT CAN BE REACHED IN NO TIME BY BIKE. STRALSUND WITH ITS BRICK GOTHIC BUILDINGS, A UNESCO WORLD HERITAGE SITE AND THE OZEANEUM ARE JUST AN HOUR DRIVE AWAY.

IN DER UMGEBUNG. VOM MICRO-HOME ZUM OSTSEESTRAND UND ZUM BODDEN SIND ES NUR WENIGE GEHMINUTEN. DAS KUNSTMUSEUM AHRENSHOOP ERREICHT MAN IN EIN PAAR MINUTEN ZU FUSS. MIT DEM FAHRRAD IST MAN IN KURZER ZEIT IM NATIONALPARK VORPOMMERSCHE BODDENLANDSCHAFT. IN NUR EINER STUNDE ERREICHT MAN MIT DEM AUTO STRALSUND MIT DEN ZUM UNESCO-WELTERBE GEHÖRENDEN BAUTEN DER BACKSTEINGOTIK UND DEM OZEANEUM.

Exterior terrace. Floor plan.
View from the garden.
Außenterrasse. Grundriss.
Ansicht vom Garten.

Interior view of the living area. Bathroom.
View from the garden.
Innenansicht Wohnbereich. Badezimmer.
Blick vom Garten.

INFORMATION. ARCHITECT>
NINA HEFFELS // 2014. 2 HOUSES>
140 SQM AND 180 SQM // 6 GUESTS
AND 8 GUESTS // 2 AND 3 BEDROOMS
// 1 BATHROOM AND 1 BATHROOM
WITH TUB AND SAUNA + 1 GUEST WC.
ADDRESS> KARBYER STRASSE 1,
BRODERSBY, GERMANY.
WWW.GUTSCHWANSEN.DE

Interior view of a bedroom. Porch.
Innenansicht Schlafzimmer. Windfang.

Gut Schwansen

BRODERSBY, GERMANY |
DEUTSCHLAND

Schwansen manor is situated in a hilly landscape, just a few minutes from the Baltic Sea and the Schlei River. Built in 1820, the thatched house has been lavishly restored and furnished to a high standard. Two large apartments are furnished in style and equipped with fireplaces, making them ideal for spending beautiful days in fall and winter. The bathrooms are modern; the larger apartment has a bathtub and a sauna. The interior blends modern and antique decor in harmony. There is direct access to roofed terraces with a gas grill, great for chilling out in the evenings or when the weather is bad, and to over 2,000 square meters of charming grounds with mature trees.

Das Reetdachanwesen Gut Schwansen liegt in hügeliger Landschaft, wenige Minuten zwischen Ostsee und der Schlei. Das im Jahre 1820 erbaute Reetdachhaus wurde aufwändig restauriert und hochwertig ausgestattet. Die zwei großzügigen Wohnungen sind stilvoll eingerichtet und mit Kamin versehen — perfekt auch für schöne Tage im Herbst und Winter. Die Bäder sind modern ausgestattet und die große Wohnung zudem mit Badewanne und Sauna. Die Möblierung mixt harmonisch modernes und antikes Interieur. Direkt anschließende, überdachte Terrassen mit Gasgrill laden abends oder bei schlechtem Wetter zum Verweilen ein. Das großzügige Grundstück von über 2.000 qm bezaubert mit altem Baumbestand.

Exterior view from the garden. Dining area.
Außenansicht vom Garten. Essbereich.

GETTING AROUND. BRODERSBY IS ONLY A FEW MINUTES AWAY FROM THE BALTIC BEACH OR THE SHORE OF THE SCHLEI RIVER. THE REGION OFFERS GREAT CYCLING PATHS, WATER SPORTS LOVERS SAVOR THE SCHLEI BY SAILBOAT OR KAYAK. THE VIKING VILLAGE OF HAITABU, GOTTORF CASTLE OR THE GELTINGER BIRK, FOR EXAMPLE, ARE WORTH DISCOVERING. AND SO IS THE CULINARY VARIETY: FROM FRESH FISH IN THE HARBOR OF KAPPEL TO GOURMET CUISINE AT GUT DAMP!

IN DER UMGEBUNG. BRODERSBY IST NUR WENIGE MINUTEN VON OSTSEE-STRAND ODER DEM UFER DER SCHLEI ENTFERNT. DIE REGION BIETET GUT AUSGEBAUTE FAHRRADWEGE, WAS-SERSPORTLER GENIESSEN DIE SCHLEI AUF DEM SEGELBOOT ODER KAJAK. ENTDECKUNGEN SIND Z. B. DAS WIK-INGER-DORF HAITABU, SCHLOSS GOT-TORF ODER DIE GELTINGER BIRK. UND AUCH DIE KULINARISCHE VIELFALT: VON FRISCHEM FISCH AM HAFEN VON KAPPELN BIS ZUR STERNENKÜCHE AUF GUT DAMP!

View of the living room. Floor plans.
Exterior view.
Blick ins Wohnzimmer. Grundrisse.
Außenansicht.

Living room. Bathroom with bathtub.
Porch and garden.
Wohnzimmer. Badezimmer mit Badewanne.
Veranda und Garten.

INFORMATION. ARCHITECT>
PETER DOBELSTEIN // INTERIOR
DESIGN > MICHAELA FASOLD
AND OLIVER FASOLD // 2016.
HOUSE> 120 SQM // 6 GUESTS //
3 BEDROOMS // 2 BATHROOMS.
ADDRESS> AM KURPARK 21,
BREEGE, GERMANY.
WW.LILLESOL.DE

*Bedroom. Interior view of the living room with
fireplace. Side view.
Schlafzimmer. Innenansicht Wohnzimmer
mit Kamin. Seitenansicht.*

Dining area. Garden.
Living room with large windows.
Essbereich. Garten.
Wohnzimmer mit großen Fenstern.

Lillesol

BREEGE, GERMANY |
DEUTSCHLAND

The Lillesol holiday home is located just a few minutes' walk from the beach at Julius von der Lancken's historic spa gardens in the Baltic resort of Juliusruh on the island of Rügen. This building stands out due to its consistent simplicity. The wood-clad structure creates an impact alone through its minimalist design language and the choice of materials and colors. The interior also reflects the principle of focusing on a calm color palette and a small selection of high-quality materials. The large windows offer views of the baroque park. A gallery creates a spacious, luminous ambience. It is made cozy by the fireplace and sauna, perfect for warming up after a walk on the beach in the cold season. Three bedrooms and two bathrooms make the house suitable for six people.

Nur wenige Gehminuten vom Strand entfernt liegt das Ferienhaus Lillesol am historischen Kurpark von Julius von der Lancken im Ostseebad Juliusruh auf Rügen. Das Gebäude fällt durch seine konsequente Schlichtheit auf. Der holzverkleidete Baukörper wirkt allein durch seine reduzierte Formensprache und die Wahl von Material und Farbe. Auch die Gestaltung der Innenräume folgt dem Prinzip der Konzentration auf eine ruhige Farbpalette und wenige, aber hochwertige Materialien. Die großen Fenster bieten Ausblicke in den barocken Park. Die Galerie schafft ein großzügiges, lichtes Ambiente. Heimelig wird es durch den Kamin und die Sauna, perfekt fürs Aufwärmen nach dem Strandspaziergang in der kalten Jahreszeit. Mit drei Schlafzimmern und zwei Bädern bietet das Haus Platz für sechs Personen.

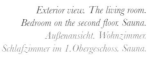

Exterior view. The living room.
Bedroom on the second floor. Sauna.
Außenansicht. Wohnzimmer.
Schlafzimmer im 1. Obergeschoss. Sauna.

GETTING AROUND. THE SANDY BEACH CALLED SCHAABE IS ONLY A FEW MINUTES' WALK AWAY. THE AREA OFFERS MANY OPTIONS FOR ACTIVITIES SUCH AS CYCLING, FISHING, HORSEBACK RIDING, SAILING AND HIKING, AND DESTINATIONS LIKE THE HIDDENSEE FERRY, THE CHALK CLIFFS, THE FISHING VILLAGE OF VITT AND THE FASHIONABLE SEASIDE RESORTS. RÜGEN AND STRALSUND, THE KÖNIGSTUHL, OR THE JASMUND NATURE PARK ARE NOT FAR AWAY EITHER.

IN DER UMGEBUNG. DER SAND-STRAND SCHAABE IST IN NUR WE-NIGEN GEHMINUTEN ERREICHBAR. AUSSERDEM SORGEN RADTOUREN, ANGELN, REITEN, SEGELN UND WAN-DERN EBENSO FÜR VIEL ABWECHS-LUNG WIE DIE FÄHRVERBINDUNG NACH HIDDENSEE, DIE KREIDEFEL-SEN, DAS FISCHERDORF VITT UND DIE MONDÄNEN SEEBÄDER. AUCH NACH RÜGEN UND STRALSUND, ZUM KÖNIGSTUHL, ODER ZUM NATURPARK JASMUND IST ES NICHT WEIT.

INFORMATION. ARCHITECTS>
PETE J.C. WELBERGEN, CLARA
WELBERGEN // 2017. MANOR
HOUSE> 890 SQM // 30 GUESTS //
10 BEDROOMS // 10 BATHROOMS.
ADDRESS> ÜSELITZ 2, POSERITZ,
RÜGEN, GERMANY.
WWW.UESELITZ.DE

Interior view of Gut Üselitz. Details.
Living area.
Innenansicht Gut Üselitz. Details.
Wohnbereich.

Gut Üselitz

RÜGEN, GERMANY |
DEUTSCHLAND

The reconstruction of the manor house, which dates back to the 16th century and is a listed building, only began in 2012. The basic idea behind the complex and careful renovation of the building was to preserve historical elements and to design new modern and distinguishable ones. The three upper floors of the manor house were transformed into seven high standard apartments, which are available for short- and medium-term rental. There are spacious rooms and other spaces on the first floor and in the manor park, which are perfect for hosting all kinds of ceremonies, retreats and other events, and are exclusively available to tenants who rent the entire house. The environment amidst the overgrown nature makes the Üselitz manor so special.

Der Wiederaufbau des aus dem 16. Jahrhundert stammenden und unter Denkmalschutz stehenden Herrenhauses begann erst 2012. Historische Elemente zu bewahren und neue Elemente modern und ablesbar zu gestalten war der Grundgedanke der aufwendigen und liebevollen Sanierung des Gebäudes. In den drei Obergeschossen des Herrenhauses wurden sieben hochwertige Wohnungen eingerichtet, die zur kurz- und mittelfristigen Nutzung angeboten werden. In Erdgeschoss und Gutspark befinden sich großzügige Räume und Flächen, die für die Ausrichtung aller denkbaren feierlichen Anlässe, Retreats und sonstigen Veranstaltungen geeignet sind und den Gästen bei Miete des ganzen Hauses exklusiv zur Verfügung stehen. Die Umgebung inmitten der wieder verwilderten Natur machen die Besonderheit von Gut Üselitz aus.

GETTING AROUND. ÜSELITZ IS SITUATED IN THE SOUTH OF THE ISLAND OF RÜGEN, WHICH HAS A WONDERFUL VAST LANDSCAPE. THE PROPERTY IS SURROUNDED ON ALL SIDES BY THE ÜSELITZER WIEK, A PROTECTED SEA BAY. SIGHTS IN THE SURROUNDINGS INCLUDE THE RÜGEN CHALK CLIFFS, THE ARCHITECTURE AROUND PRORA AND THE CONCRETE BUILDING DESIGNED BY ULRICH MÜTHER IN BINZ. ESPECIALLY RECOMMENDED ARE THE CONCERT SERIES IN SPRING AND SUMMER.

IN DER UMGEBUNG. ÜSELITZ LIEGT IM SÜDEN DER INSEL RÜGEN, WELCHE EINE WUNDERBARE WEITE LAND-SCHAFT BIETET. DAS GRUNDSTÜCK IST VON ALLEN SEITEN DURCH DIE ÜSELIT-ZER WIEK, EINE UNTER NATURSCHUTZ STEHENDE MEERESBUCHT, UMGE-BEN. SEHENSWÜRDIGKEITEN IN DER UMGEBUNG UMFASSEN DIE RÜGENER KREIDEFELSEN, DIE ARCHITEKTUR UM PRORA UND DEN BETONBAU VON UL-RICH MÜTHER IN BINZ. BESONDERS ZU EMPFEHLEN SIND DIE FESTSPIELFRÜH-LING UND FESTSPIELSOMMER.

Interior view. First floor and
second floor plan. Üselitz Park.
Innenansicht. Grundrisse Erdgeschoss und
1.Obergeschoss. Üselitz Park.

Interior view of the living area. Dining area.
Üselitz manor and surroundings from above.
Innenansicht Wohnbereich. Essbereich.
Gut Üselitz und Umgebung von oben.

INFORMATION. ARCHITECT>
MARTIN FOCKS // 2004.
5 HOUSES WITH 14 APARTMENTS>
65, 70 AND 100 SQM // 64 GUESTS //
FROM 1 TO 3 BEDROOMS
EACH APARTMENT // FROM
1 TO 2 BATHROOMS EACH.
ADDRESS> TRIFTWEG 1 C,
KÖLPINSEE, GERMANY.
WWW.SCHWEDEN-ROT.DE

Exterior view. View from the garden.
Living room. Schwedenrot.
Außenansicht. Blick vom Garten.
Wohnzimmer. Schwedenrot.

Schwedenrot

KÖLPINSEE, GERMANY |
DEUTSCHLAND

Five wooden houses painted in original Swedish red stand on a small light hill surrounded by pine trees, rowan trees and sea buckthorn. Simply reduced and furnished, the whole day can be spent relaxing in Schwedenrot: Having breakfast on the terrace, relaxing in the evening in the sauna or getting together in a cozy atmosphere around the Swedish stove. All apartments are bright and modern, accessible at ground level or via ramps, and most of them are barrier-free. By the favorable situation of the holiday homes the beach, railroad station, bicycle rental, riding stable and restaurants are well accessible both on foot and by bicycle.

In original Schwedenrot gestrichen, stehen fünf mit Holz verkleidete Häuser auf einem kleinen lichten Hügel, umgeben von Kiefern, Ebereschen und Sanddorn. Schlicht reduziert und eingerichtet lässt sich der ganze Tag erholsam im Schwedenrot verbringen: Frühstück auf der Terrasse, Entspannen am Abend in der Sauna oder gemütliches Beisammensein am Schwedenofen. Die hellen und modern ausgestatteten Wohnungen sind ebenerdig oder über Rampen zu erreichen und überwiegend barrierefrei gebaut. Durch die günstige Lage der Ferienwohnungen lassen sich Strand, Bahnhof, Fahrradverleih, Reiterhof und Restaurants gut zu Fuß oder per Fahrrad erreichen.

Exterior view from the garden.
Interior view.
Außenansicht vom Garten.
Innenansicht.

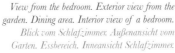

View from the bedroom. Exterior view from the garden. Dining area. Interior view of a bedroom.
Blick vom Schlafzimmer. Außenansicht vom Garten. Essbereich. Inneansicht Schlafzimmer.

GETTING AROUND. THE NATURE RESERVE LODDINER HÖFT OFFERS A BEAUTIFUL VIEW OVER THE BACKWATERS. THE 42 KILOMETER LONG SANDY BEACH IS PERFECT FOR LONG WALKS AND IN SUMMER FOR SWIMMING. THE ISLAND IS BEST TO EXPLORE FROM THE SCHWEDENROT BY BIKE ON GOOD CYCLING PATHS AND WITHOUT A CAR.

IN DER UMGEBUNG. IM NATUR-SCHUTZGEBIET LODDINER HÖFT ERWARTET SIE EIN WUNDERSCHÖ-NER BLICK ÜBER DAS ACHTERWASSER. DER 42 KILOMETER LANGE SAND-STRAND LÄDT ZU LANGEN SPAZIER-GÄNGEN EIN UND IM SOMMER ZUM BADEN. AUF GUT AUSGEBAUTEN RADWEGEN IST DIE INSEL BESTENS OHNE AUTO VOM SCHWEDENROT AUS ZU ERKUNDEN.

INFORMATION. ARCHITECTS>
NORM ARCHITECTS AND MENU//
1918 FORMER MERCHANT HOUSE,
2019 RENOVATION. HOTEL>
2,200 SQM // CA. 20 GUESTS //
10 BEDROOMS // 1 BATHROOM EACH.
ADDRESS> NORDHAVN,
COPENHAGEN, DENMARK.
WWW.THFAUDO.COM

*A bedroom. Exterior view
of the former merchant house.
Interior view.
Schlafzimmer. Außenansicht
des ehemaligen Kaufmannshauses.
Innenansicht.*

The Audo

COPENHAGEN, DENMARK |
DÄNEMARK

Being a hybrid space, The Audo serves several functions: as a hotel residence, café, concept store, material library, creative workspace and event space, The Audo unites all uses under its roof. The 10-room hotel is secluded on the top floor of the former merchant's house in Nordhavn, and offers unobtrusive and intimate retreats in loft style. The cozy yet spacious rooms are decorated beneath their wooden beams with carefully selected objects and artwork. Natural materials and high-quality Danish design characterize the rooms.

Als hybrider Raum bietet The Audo verschiedene Funktionen: als Hotel-residenz, Café, Concept Store, Materialbibliothek, kreativer Arbeits- und Veranstaltungsraum vereint The Audo alle Nutzungen unter seinem Dach. Das 10-Zimmer-Hotel liegt versteckt im obersten Stockwerk des ehemaligen Kaufmannshauses in Nordhavn und bietet unaufdringliche und intime Rückzugsmöglichkeiten im Loft-Stil. Die gemütlichen und dennoch geräumigen Zimmer sind mit sorgfältig ausgewählten Objekten und Kunstwerken unter den freiliegenden Holzbalken gestaltet. Natürliche Materialien und hochwertiges dänisches Design prägen die Räume.

GETTING AROUND. NORDHAVN HAS BECOME A HOT SPOT BY THE WATER FOR ARCHITECTURE LOVERS. YOU CAN EXPLORE THE AREA WITH THE HOTEL'S OWN RENTAL BICYCLES. THE CROISSANT AND SOURDOUGH BREAD AT THE LOCAL BAKERY ANDERSEN & MAILLARD ARE HIGHLY RECOMMENDED!

IN DER UMGEBUNG. NORDHAVN HAT SICH FÜR ARCHITEKTURLIEBHA-BER ZU EINEM HOTSPOT AM WASSER ENTWICKELT. ERKUNDEN LÄSST SICH DAS AREAL MIT DEN HOTELEIGENEN LEIHFAHRRÄDERN. BEI DER LOKALEN BÄCKEREI ANDERSEN & MAILLARD SIND BESONDERS DIE CROISSANT UND DAS SAUERTEIGBROT ZU EMP-FEHLEN!

Interior view of a hotel room. Living area.
The common area.
Innenansicht Hotelzimmer. Wohnbereich.
Gemeinschaftsbereich.

Sleeping area. Interior view.
Detail custom-made wooden furniture.
Schlafbereich. Innenansicht.
Detail maßgefertigte Holzmöbel.

INFORMATION. ARCHITECT>
ELIZABETH BUCHNER SCHLÖGL //
2007. 2 HOUSES> 184 SQM BOTH //
5 GUESTS PER HOUSE // 2 BEDROOMS
EACH // 1 BATHROOM EACH.
ADDRESS> ZUM MÖWENORT 18,
LÜTOW, GERMANY.
WWW.USEDOM-RELAXX.DE

Exterior view Usedom-Relaxx. Sourroundings.
Interior view of the kitchen area.
Außenansicht Usedom-Relaxx. Umgebung.
Innenansicht Küchenbereich.

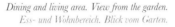
Dining and living area. View from the garden.
Ess- und Wohnbereich. Blick vom Garten.

Usedom-Relaxx

LÜTOW, GERMANY |
DEUTSCHLAND

Modern comfort reigns in the two houses, that are embedded in greenery only a short walk from the backwaters of Usedom. This is achieved by combining minimalist, modern furniture with wooden floors and ceilings of a warm tone. Plus, lots of light flooding the rooms through the large windows, fireplaces for the cold season and kitchens and bathrooms equipped to a particularly high standard. Both parts of the house have a private garden section, and the bathhouse with sauna and whirlpool can be booked on request.

In den zwei Hausteilen, die eingebettet in viel Grün nur ein paar Minuten zu Fuß vom Usedomer Achterwasser entfernt liegen, herrscht moderne Behaglichkeit. Das gelingt hier mit reduzierter, moderner Einrichtung, die mit warm anmutenden Holzböden- und Decken kombiniert wird. Dazu viel Licht, das durch die großen Fensterfronten in die Räume strahlt, Kaminfeuer für die kalte Jahreszeit und besonders hochwertig ausgestattete Küchen und Bäder. Beide Hausteile haben einen eigenen Gartenteil, auf Wunsch kann das Badehaus mit Sauna und Whirlpool mitgebucht werden.

*Exterior view. Relaxation area with
pool. Detail of the living room.*
*Ansicht von außen. Entspannungsbereich mit
Becken. Detail Wohnzimmer.*

GETTING AROUND. THE SUMMER
BEACH CHAIR IN ZINNOWITZ AND
BICYCLES ARE ALL INCLUDED,
BECAUSE NOTHING IN USEDOM
FEELS MORE NATURAL THAN
ENJOYING THE BEACH OR EXPLORING
THE ISLAND BY BIKE: THE NATURE
RESERVE WITH ITS 32-METER-HIGH
CLIFFS, EXTENSIVE JUNIPER AND PINE
FORESTS, AND WETLAND BIOTOPES.

IN DER UMGEBUNG. DER SOMMER-
STRANDKORB IN ZINNOWITZ UND
FAHRRÄDER SIND BEI DER BUCHUNG
INKLUSIVE – DENN NICHTS LIEGT AUF
USEDOM NÄHER, ALS DEN STRAND
ZU GENIESSEN ODER DIE INSEL PER
FAHRRAD ZU ERKUNDEN: DAS NATUR-
SCHUTZGEBIET MIT SEINER 32 METER
HOHEN STEILKÜSTE, AUSGEDEHNTE
WACHHOLDER - UND KIEFERNWÄLDER
UND FEUCHTBIOTOPE.

Sauna. Bedroom with garden view.
Sauna. Schlafzimmer mit Blick auf den Garten.

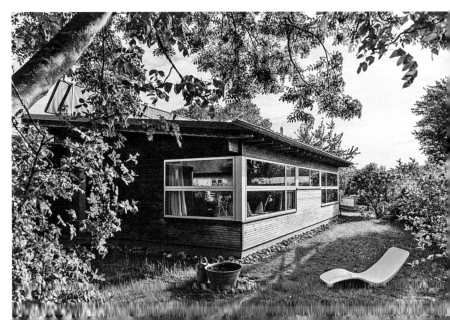

Bedroom with single beds.
Exterior view from the garden.
Schlafzimmer mit Einzelbetten.
Außenansicht vom Garten.

INFORMATION. ARCHITECTS> ARCHITEKTURBÜRO GRIEBEL // 2018. 8 HOUSES> 4 HOUSES OF CA. 85 SQM AND 4 OF CA. 65 SQM // 2–6 GUESTS // 4 HOUSES WITH 2 BEDROOMS AND 4 WITH 1 BEDROOM // 4 HOUSES WITH 2 BATHROOMS AND 4 WITH 1 BATHROOM. ADDRESS> FEHMARNSUND 34, FEHMARN, GERMANY. WWW.THEVILLAS.DE

Living and dining area of villa White II.
Detail bedroom.
Wohn- und Essbereich Villa White II.
Detail Schlafzimmer.

The Villas

FEHMARN, GERMANY |
DEUTSCHLAND

The ensemble of eight beach villas in Scandinavian style is right by the sea on the island of Fehmarn – the sound of the waves is included! The bedrooms on the glazed second floors provide unobstructed views of the sky, the Baltic Sea and the beach. All villas are modern and designed with great attention to detail. The scene for a relaxing break is set by bright open-plan kitchens, high-end furnishings, stoves and roof terraces with dream view. Each of the boutique beach houses has an outdoor sauna that offers panoramic views of the nature reserve with Dexter cattle, deer and pheasants.

Das Ensemble von acht Strandvillen in skandinavischem Design liegt direkt am Meer auf der Insel Fehmarn – Meeresrauschen inklusive! Die Schlafzimmer in den verglasten Obergeschossen haben freie Sicht auf den Himmel, die Ostsee und den Strand. Alle Villen sind mit viel Liebe zum Detail konzipiert und modern eingerichtet. Helle Wohnküchen, hochwertige Ausstattung, Kaminöfen und die Dachterrassen mit Traumblick bilden die Szenerie für entspannte Urlaubstage. Die Boutique-Strandhäuser werden durch eine Außensauna mit Panoramablick in das Naturschutzgebiet mit Dexter Rindern, Rehen und Fasanen ergänzt.

Exterior view from the front through the beach grass.
Kitchen of villa Gold I.

Außenansicht von vorne durch den Strandhafer.
Küche Villa Gold I.

GETTING AROUND. FEHMARN'S 78 KILOMETERS OF COASTLINE AND 20 BEACHES ATTRACT WALKERS, ANGLERS, AND WATER SPORTS ENTHUSIASTS SUCH AS WINDSURFERS OR KITE SURFERS. THE GOLF COURSE IS ONLY A FEW MINUTES AWAY AND FEHMARN'S CITY CENTER BURG IS ALSO CLOSE BY. IT IS WORTH VISITING THE GALILEO WISSENSWELT AND THE BUTTERFLY PARK.

IN DER UMGEBUNG. FEHMARNS 78 KÜSTENKILOMETER UND 20 STRÄNDE LOCKEN SPAZIERGÄNGER, ANGLER UND WASSERSPORTLER WIE WIND- ODER KITESURFER. DER GOLFPLATZ IST NUR EIN PAAR MINUTEN ENTFERNT UND AUCH FEHMARNS STADTZEN-TRUM BURG IST SCHNELL ERREICHT. HIER LOHNT SICH EIN BESUCH DER GALILEO WISSENSWELT UND DES SCHMETTERLINGSPARKS.

Dining area of villa White I. Floor plans
of villa White II and Gold I.
Living and dining area of villa Azure I.
Essbereich Villa White I. Grundrisse
Villa White II und Villa Gold I.
Wohn- und Essbereich Villa Azure I.

Interior view bathroom. Living room of villa Gold I.
Bedroom on the second floor of villa Gold I.
Innenansicht Bad. Wohnzimmer Villa Gold I.
Schlafzimmer 1.Obergeschoss Villa Gold I.

INFORMATION. ARCHITECTS>
ARCGENCY // 2017. RETREAT>
166 SQM + 120 SQM TERRACE //
2 GUESTS // 1 BEDROOM //
1 BATHROOM + SPA.
ADDRESS> SKUDEHAVNSVEJ 1,
NORDHAVN, COPENHAGEN,
DENMARK.
WWW.THEKRANE.DK

THEKRANE from top. Exterior view.
Interior view of the lounge.
THEKRANE von oben. Außenansicht.
Innenansicht Lounge.

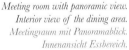

Meeting room with panoramic view.
Interior view of the dining area.
Meetingraum mit Panoramablick.
Innenansicht Essbereich.

THEKRANE

COPENHAGEN, DENMARK |
DÄNEMARK

In the former coal crane in Copenhagen's Nordhavn is a one-room hotel with panoramic views of the sea, sky, harbor, and city. The room in the old engine room has a minimalist interior with functional furniture and high-quality materials. The custom-made furniture is designed to integrate the beds, seating, and wardrobes into wall panels. The all-black interior and black-painted walls, floors and ceilings create a sense of intimacy and tranquility and set the stage for the extraordinary view. In contrast to the black interior of THEKRANEROOM, the spa below is designed in lighter tones and is generously clad in light stone. Terraces and a small lounge are unique vantage points, exclusive to visitors.

Im ehemaligen Kohlekran im Kopenhagener Nordhavn befindet sich ein Ein-Zimmer-Hotel mit Panoramablick über Meer, Himmel, Hafen und Stadt. Das Zimmer im alten Maschinenraum hat eine minimalistische Einrichtung mit funktionalen Möbeln und hochwertigen Materialien. Die maßgefertigten Möbel sind so konstruiert, dass die Betten, Sitzgelegenheiten und Schränke in Wandpaneele integriert sind. Das ganz in Schwarz gehaltene Interieur und die schwarzen Wände, Böden und Decken schaffen ein Gefühl von Intimität und Ruhe und bilden den Rahmen für die besondere Aussicht. Im Gegensatz zum schwarzen Interieur des THEKRANE-ROOM ist das unten gelegene Spa heller gestaltet und großflächig mit hellem Stein verkleidet. Terrassen und eine kleine Lounge sind einzigartige Aussichtspunkte, exklusiv für die Besucher.

Exterior view. Spa with panoramic view.
Detail of the glass front. Interior view.
Floor plans.
Außenansicht. Spa mit Panoramablick.
Detail der Glasfassade. Innenansicht.
Grundrisse.

GETTING AROUND. THE CONSTANT-LY TRANSFORMING AREA OF THE INDUSTRIAL HARBOR NORDHAVN STILL HAS ITS ORIGINAL INDUSTRIAL CHARM ALONGSIDE SEVERAL NEW BUILDINGS. THE REFFEN AREA WITH A LARGE STREET FOOD MARKET IS NOT FAR AWAY. THE CONTEMPORARY COPENHAGEN MUSEUM SHOWS EXHIBITIONS IN FORMER FACTORY BUILDINGS.

IN DER UMGEBUNG. DAS SICH STÄN-DIG VERÄNDERNDE AREAL DES INDUS-TRIEHAFENS NORDHAVN HAT NEBEN VIELEN NEUBAUTEN AUCH NOCH IMMER EINEN URSPRÜNGLICHEN INDUSTRIELLEN CHARME. NICHT WEIT ENTFERNT LIEGT DAS AREAL REFFEN MIT GROSSEM STREET FOOD MARKT. DAS MUSEUM COPENHAGEN CONT-EMPORARY ZEIGT AUSSTELLUNGEN IN ALTEN INDUSTRIEHALLEN.

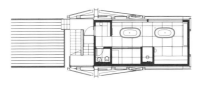
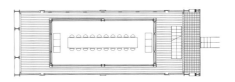
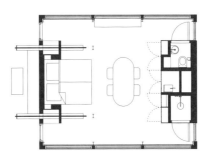

INFORMATION. ARCHITECTS>
HONKA HAUS FINNLAND //
1979, RENOVATION 2021.
BLOCKHOUSE> 57 SQM // 4 GUESTS //
2 BEDROOMS // 1 BATHROOM.
ADDRESS> FLADENWEG 29,
BRODERSBY-GOLTOFT, GERMANY.
WWW.HAUSZWEINEUN.DE

*Front view from street. Fireplace in the open
living-dining area. View from the gallery to the
dining table on the first floor.
Vorderansicht von der Straße. Kaminofen im offenem
Wohn- Essbereich. Blick von der Galerie auf den
Esstisch im Erdgeschoss.*

HAUS
ZWEINEUN

BRODERSBY, GERMANY |
DEUTSCHLAND

The vacation home HAUS ZWEINEUN
has been remodeled and furnished in a
careful and individual way, putting a lot
of emphasis on the preservation of the
characteristic and unique architecture
of the Honka log house from the 1970s.
The open first floor area with kitchen
and counter, the large dining table, and
the cozy fireplace area with ground level
access to the two terraces offers plenty of
space for joint activities while giving everyone enough freedom. All furnishings,
home accessories, coffee table books,
books and paintings have been compiled
with love and in a truly original way.
The house's inspiring and idyllic setting,
being so close to the water and in such a
peaceful location, is instantly captivating
guests.

Das Ferienhaus HAUS ZWEINEUN
wurde behutsam und individuell umgestaltet und eingerichtet, dabei wurde
viel Wert auf den Erhalt der charakte-
ristischen und besonderen Architektur
des Honka-Blockhauses aus den
1970er-Jahren gelegt. Der offen gehaltene Erdgeschossbereich mit Küche
und Esstheke, dem großzügigen Esstisch
und der gemütlichen Kaminecke mit
ebenerdigem Zugang zu den beiden
Terrassen bietet viel Platz für gemein-
same Aktivitäten und lässt dennoch
für jeden Gast genug Freiraum.
Alle Einrichtungsgegenstände. Wohn-
Accessoires, Bildbände, Bücher und
Gemälde sind liebevoll und einzigartig
zusammengestellt worden. Die inspirie-
rende Idylle dieses Hauses, so nah am
Wasser und so ruhig gelegen, zieht die
Gäste sofort in ihren Bann.

GETTING AROUND. THE IMMEDIATE PROXIMITY TO THE SCHLEI RIVER GIVES A WIDE RANGE OF OPTIONS: KITING, CANOEING, SAILING ON THE WATER AND ENJOY THE SMALL BEACHES. IN CLOSE VICINITY, AND IN EASY REACH ARE PLACES TO VISIT SUCH AS THE GOTTORF CASTLE MUSEUM, THE NOLDE MUSEUM, THE VIKING MUSEUM HAITHABU OR THE CITIES OF SCHLESWIG, ECKERNFÖRDE, FLENSBURG AND HUSUM.

IN DER UMGEBUNG. DIE UNMIT-TELBARE NÄHE ZUR SCHLEI BIETET VIELFÄLTIGE ANGEBOTE: AUF DEM WASSER KITEN, KANUFAHREN, SEGELN UND DIE KLEINEN STRÄNDE GENIES-SEN. IN DER NAHEN UMGEBUNG SIND AUSFLUGSZIELE WIE DAS MUSEUM SCHLOSS GOTTORF, DAS NOLDE MUSEUM, DAS WIKINGER MUSEUM HAITHABU ODER DIE STÄDTE SCHLES-WIG, ECKERNFÖRDE, FLENSBURG UND HUSUM GUT ZU ERREICHEN.

Bright and open living/dining area. Sitting area on the large, covered terrace. Gallery with sleeping accommodation for two people.
Offener und heller Wohn- Essbereich. Sitzbereich auf der großen überdachten Terrasse. Galerie mit Schlafgelegenheit für zwei Personen.

Bedroom on the first floor with a collection's pictures gallery.
View of the gallery and staircase.
View over the grass of the dunes to the Schlei.
Schlafzimmer im Erdgeschoss mit Bildergalerie aus Sammlung.
Ansicht auf Galeriebord und Treppe.
Blick über das Dünengras auf die Schlei.

INFORMATION. ARCHITECT>
THOMAS SANDELL // 2020.
HOUSE> 50 SQM AND 15 SQM
TERRACE // 4 GUESTS // 1 BEDROOM.
ADDRESS> GUÖVIKSVÄGEN 353,
TRENSUM, SWEDEN.
WWW1.ERIKSBERG.SE/EN/C-ROOMS-
SUITES/SYNVILLAN

SynVillan exterior view. Detail from below.
Interior view of a bedroom.
Außenansicht SynVillan. Detail von unten.
Innenansicht Schlafzimmer.

SynVillan - The Illusion Villa

TRENSUM, SWEDEN | SCHWEDEN

It is truly unique to experience nature and architecture right at the heart of the Eriksberg nature and safari park: SynVillan is suspended on stilts, three meters above the ground. Based on the shape of a traditional Swedish house with a thatched roof, it has a surprising façade clad in polished steel plates. Reflections of light create the illusion of a dissolving structure. The house is easily accessible via a staircase. On 50 square meters for up to four people, there are two light-flooded, bright, and modern furnished rooms and a kitchenette. A fireplace stove provides coziness, and both from the terrace and from several panorama windows you can overlook the Baltic sea and the beautiful nature park's expanse.

Inmitten des Natur- und Safariparks Eriksberg lässt sich Natur und Architektur ganz besonders erleben: SynVillan schwebt auf Pfählen, drei Meter über dem Boden. In seiner Form an das traditionelle schwedische Haus angelehnt und mit Reet eingedeckt, überrascht die Fassade, die mit polierten Stahlplatten verkleidet ist. Die Lichtreflexionen erzeugen die Illusion eines sich auflösenden Baukörpers. Das Haus ist bequem über ein Treppe zu erreichen. Auf 50 qm für bis zu vier Personen finden sich zwei lichtdurchflutete, hell und modern möblierte Zimmer und eine Kochnische. Ein Kaminofen sorgt für Gemütlichkeit und von der Terrasse und durch verschiedene Panoramafenster überblickt man die Ostsee und die Weite des schönen Naturparks.

Exterior view in the evening.
Bedroom with single beds.
Außenansicht mit Abendstimmung.
Schlafzimmer mit Einzelbetten.

*Panorama from terrace. Living room
atmosphere in the evening. Detail fireplace.
SynVillan from below.
Panorama von Terrasse. Wohnzimmer
mit Abendstimmung. Detail Kamin.
SynVillan von unten.*

GETTING AROUND. THE MAIN
ATTRACTION OF THIS PLACE IS TO
EXPERIENCE NATURE IN A VERY
UNIQUE WAY: THE SYNVILLAN HOVERS
DIRECTLY ABOVE A FEEDING STATION,
WHERE THE ANIMALS COME TO EAT.
A GLASS PANEL IN THE FLOOR OF
THE HOUSE MAKES IT POSSIBLE TO
OBSERVE RED AND FALLOW DEER,
BISON, WILD BOAR AND MOUFLON.
THE NATURE PARK CAN BE EXPLORED
ON GUIDED TOURS BY BIKE OR JEEP.

IN DER UMGEBUNG. HIER STEHT
DAS BESONDERE NATURERLEBNIS IM
FOCUS: DAS SYNVILLAN SCHWEBT
DIREKT ÜBER EINER FUTTERSTEL-
LE, ZU DER DIE TIERE ZUM FRESSEN
KOMMEN. DURCH EINE GLASPLATTE
IM BODEN DES HAUSES LASSEN SICH
ROT- UND DAMHIRSCHE, WISENTE,
WILDSCHWEINE UND MUFFLONS
BEOBACHTEN. AUF GEFÜHRTEN
TOUREN PER FAHRRAD ODER JEEP
KANN DER NATURPARK WEITER ER-
KUNDET WERDEN.

INFORMATION. ARCHITECT> ANDREAS BRECKWOLDT // 2006. GRANARY WITH 4 APARTMENTS> 1,200 SQM // 34 GUESTS // 16 BEDROOMS // 10 BATHROOMS. ADDRESS> ZICKER 16, ZUDAR AUF RÜGEN, GERMANY. WWW.KORNSPEICHER-MAURITZ.DE

Living area with fireplace.
Interior view.
Wohnbereich mit Kamin.
Innenansicht.

Kornspeicher Mauritz

ZUDAR AUF RÜGEN, GERMANY |
DEUTSCHLAND

The 100-year-old granary was carefully renovated over a period of two years and converted to apartments. Since 2006, this former granary contains four light-flooded, large vacation homes. A large 500-square-meter apartment with eight bedrooms, four bathrooms, a large living room with a cooking island and a large dining table is at the core of the complex. The Loft apartment located in the former barn comes with floor heating, a cooking island and access to the garden. The apartments upstairs reflect the nature of the historic building with its old beams. There is a large garden with fruit trees, plenty of space and a small pool. On cool days a small community sauna provides cozy warmth. All apartments have balconies or terraces with beautiful views.

Der 100 Jahre alte Kornspeicher wurde zwei Jahre lang liebevoll saniert und zu Wohnzwecken umgestaltet. Seit 2006 befinden sich vier lichtdurchflutete, große Ferienwohnungen in dem ehemaligen Speicher. Kernstück bildet die große Ferienwohnung mit 500 qm, 8 Schlafzimmern, 4 Bädern, einem großen Wohnraum mit Kochinsel und großem Esstisch. In dem ehemaligen Stall befindet sich die Loft-Wohnung mit Fußbodenheizung, Kochinsel und Gartenzugang. Die oberen Wohnungen spiegeln den Charakter des historischen Gebäudes mit seinen alten Balken wider. Ein großer Garten bietet neben Obstbäumen viel Platz und einen kleinen Pool. An kühlen Tagen sorgt eine kleine Gemeinschafts-Sauna für gemütliche Wärme. Alle Wohnungen verfügen über Balkone oder Terrassen mit schönen Ausblicken.

Kornspeicher Mauritz from the garden.
Interior view of the living area.
Kornspeicher Mauritz vom Garten.
Innenansicht Wohnbereich.

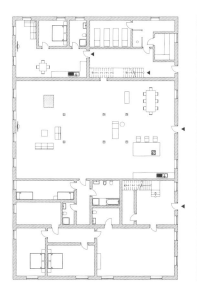

GETTING AROUND. THE KORN-SPEICHER MAURITZ IS LOCATED IN THE SOUTH OF THE ISLAND OF RÜGEN. THE HANSEATIC CITY OF STRALSUND AND THE LARGE BATHING BEACHES ARE WITHIN 30 MINUTES DISTANCE OR THE WHITE TOWN OF PUTBUS WITH THE PORT OF LAUTERBACH IS ONLY 15 MINUTES AWAY. IT IS EASY TO GET TO SPOTS FOR KITING, SAILING, WAKEBOARD-ING, HORSEBACK RIDING AND GOLFING. SWIMMING, JOGGING, HIKING AND CYCLING IS POSSIBLE RIGHT ALL AROUND THE HOUSE.

IN DER UMGEBUNG. DER KORNSPEI-CHER MAURITZ LIEGT IM SÜDEN DER INSEL RÜGEN. VON HIER ERREICHT MAN IN CA. 30 MINUTEN DIE HAN-SESTADT STRALSUND, DIE GROSSEN BADESTRÄNDE ODER IN NUR 15 MI-NUTEN DIE WEISSE STADT PUTBUS MIT DEM HAFEN LAUTERBACH. GUT ZU ERREICHEN SIND PLÄTZE ZUM KITEN, SEGELN, WAKEBOARDEN, REITEN UND GOLFEN. SCHWIMMEN, JOGGEN, WANDERN UND RAD FAHREN KANN MAN RUND UM DAS HAUS.

Dining and living area. Floor plans.
Interior view of the kitchen.
Ess- und Wohnbereich. Grundrisse.
Innenansicht Küche.

View of the living room.
A bathroom. A bedroom.
Blick zum Wohnzimmer.
Badezimmer. Schlafzimmer.

INFORMATION. ARCHITECT>
LEIF JORGENSEN // 2018. HOUSES>
BARN HOUSE 290 SQM AND FARM
HOUSE 150 SQM // 14 GUESTS //
7 BEDROOMS // 3 BATHROOMS.
ADDRESS> HØVE, ODSHERRED,
DENMARK.
WWW.LEIFJORGENSEN.COM

*Barn House interior view of the kitchen.
Entrance. Barn House living room with
panoramic window.
Innenansicht Küche Barn House.
Eingang. Wohnzimmer mit
Panoramafenster Barn House.*

Barn House and Farm House

ODSHERRED, DENMARK |
DÄNEMARK

The complex of historic and modern houses is situated at a high altitude and has a fantastic view of the Sejerø Bay. The romantic Farm House with thatched roof has been renovated in a modern style with bright elements – new pale timber panels and old timber ceilings complement each other harmoniously. There is plenty of space and five bedrooms to accommodate even large groups. The new Barn House reinterprets old techniques: it has whitewashed brick walls, and a hidden steel structure, a large living room, and three bedrooms. A two-story room that includes a kitchen, two sofa groups, a dining table for fourteen people and a fireplace is the house's center. The ceiling of up to 6.5 meters sets the feeling of space, large, glazed doorways bring a lot of light into the rooms.

Das historisch und moderne Haus-Ensemble ist hochgelegen, mit einem fantastischen Blick auf die Sejerø-Bucht. Das romantische Farm House mit Strohdach wurde modern und hell saniert – neue helle Holzvertäfelungen und alte Holzbalkendecken ergänzen sich hier harmonisch. Viel Platz und fünf Schlafzimmer laden auch große Gruppen ein. Das neue Barn House interpretiert alte Techniken neu: Es hat gekalkte Backsteinwände und eine versteckte Stahlkonstruktion, ein großes Wohn- und drei Schlafzimmer. Mittelpunkt des Hauses ist ein zweistöckiger Raum, der eine Küche, zwei Sofagruppen, einen Esstisch für 14 Personen und einen Kamin umfasst. Die Deckenhöhe von bis zu 6,5 Metern bestimmt das Raumgefühl, große verglaste Türöffnungen lassen viel Licht in die Räume.

GETTING AROUND. THE HOUSES ARE LOCATED ON HILLY TERRAIN, SURROUNDED BY BEAUTIFUL AND HISTORIC NATURE. DISCOVER BIRDLIFE, BURIAL MOUNDS FROM THE BRONZE AGE AND THE NEARBY WOOD. CYCLISTS AND HIKERS WILL FIND BEAUTIFUL ROUTES, A NUMBER OF ATTRACTIVE BATHING BEACHES ARE ONLY ABOUT 1 KILOMETER AWAY.

IN DER UMGEBUNG. DIE HÄUSER STEHEN AUF HÜGELIGEM GELÄN-DE, INMITTEN DER SCHÖNEN UND HISTORISCHEN NATUR. ENTDECKEN SIE DIE VOGELWELT, GRABHÜGEL AUS DER BRONZEZEIT UND DEN NAHE GELEGENEN WALD. RADFAHRER UND WANDERER FINDEN HIER SCHÖNE STRECKEN, EINE REIHE ATTRAKTIVER BADESTRÄNDE SIND NUR CA. 1 KM ENTFERNT.

Exterior view from the garden. Floor plan.
Barn House bedroom.
Außenansicht vom Garten. Grundriss.
Schlafzimmer Barn House.

Farm House living room with sitting area.
The Farm House kitchen. Farm House interior view.
Wohnbereich mit Sitzecke Farm House.
Küche Farm House. Innenansicht Farm House.

Map of the Baltic Sea
Ostseekarte

Picture Credits
Bildnachweis

Agentur Dreipunkt, Marco Wallberg   50–53

Simone Ahlers for JOI-Design, Hamburg   137 b. r.

Matthias Arndt, Hamburg   110–113

Max Bechmann / CATS & DOGS   114–115, 117 a. r., 117 b. l.

Ruben Beilby   38–41

BEISSERT + GRUSS ARCHITEKTEN BDA   54–56, 57 b. l.

Jonas Bjerre-Poulsen   158–160, 161 l., 161 b. r.

Irina Boersma   9 b. r., 186–189

Boje06   116

Christian Börner, Dresden   42–45

Martin Böttcher, Hamburg   106–109

Peter Carlsson   102–103, 105

Jonas Danholt for KAJ Hotel Aps   9 l., 34–37

Michael Dewanger   28 a., 29 a. l. and a. r.

Dirk Diessel, Meerane   138 l., 139–141

Sebastian Fengler   57 a. l. and r., 57 b. r.

Ferienhäuser Schloss Gelting   98–99, 100 b., 101

Focks   90–93, 154–157

Görgens   166–169

Rieke Güntsche Architekten BDA, Mainz   82–85

Gut Nehmten   26–27, 28 b., 29 b.

Oliver Hartmann, Blieskastel   29 b. r.

HAUS ZWEINEUN   174 l., 177 a. l., 177 b. r. and l.

Gregor Herberholz, Berlin   138 r., 139

Rasmus Hjortshøj - COAST Studio / Arcgency   170–173

Herbert Hofmann   65 a. r.

Holmris B8   122–125

Courtesy Hotel Sanders, Copenhagen   86–89

Malte Jaeger for Usedom-Relaxx   162–165

Ole Jais   104

Christiane Koch Fotografie   118–121

Elena Krämer Fotografie   66–69, 70–73, 130 l., 131–133

Nico Krauss   126–129

Soeren Larsen   62–64, 65 a. l., 65 b. r.

Åke E:son Lindman   14–17

Stefan Melchior   130 r.

Stefan Melchior for Michaela and Oliver Fasold   146–149

Ulrike Meutzner   9 a. r., 153

Peter Mühlhausen - Hotel Alexandra, Copenhagen   78 r.

Norm Architects   158–161

Kai Ohl   94–97

Syrine Pallisby   65 b. l.

PantherMedia / Kay Augustin   100 a.

Lars Pillmann   182–185

Bent Raj - Hotel Alexandra, Copenhagen   78 l., 80 b., 81 b. l., 81 a. r.

Laura Repp / dasmaedchenmitdemperlenohrring   117 a. l., 117 b. r.

André Reuter & Styling Miriam Hannemann   8 l., 174 r., 175–176, 177 b. l.

Anja Richter, Hamburg   22–25

Robert Rieger   150–152

SALTY Interior   30–33

Simon Schmalhort   10–13

Camilla Schmidt - CSCO.   74–77

Søren Solkær - Hotel Alexandra, Copenhagen   79, 80 a., 81 a. l.

Jan Søndergaard - Hotel Alexandra, Copenhagen   81 b. r.

Monica Grue Steffensen   161 a. r.

Nina Struwe   58–61

ulrich-fotodesign, Rostock   134–136, 137 l. and a. r.

Vipp AS   8 r., 46–49

Kersten Weichbrodt   142–145

Angelica Zander   178–181

Rozbeh Zavari   18–21

All other pictures were made available by the architects, designers, or hosts.

Cover front: Angelica Zander
Cover back (from left to right, from above to below): Gut Nehmten, Rasmus Hjortshøj - COAST Studio / Arcgency, Elena Krämer Fotografie, Ferienhäuser Schloss Gelting